PRESSURE
POINT
FIGHTING

Disclaimer: Please note that the publisher and author(s) of this instructional book are NOT RESPONSIBLE in any manner whatsoever for any injury that may result from practicing the techniques and/or following the instructions given within. Martial arts training can be dangerous—both to you and to others—if not practiced safely. If you're in doubt as to how to proceed or whether your practice is safe, consult with a trained martial arts teacher before beginning. Since the physical activities described herein may be too strenuous in nature for some readers, it is also essential that a physician be consulted prior to training.

PRESSURE POINT FIGHTING

A Guide to Striking Vital Points for Martial Arts and Self-Defense

RICK CLARK

TUTTLE Publishing

Tokyo | Rutland, Vermont | Singapore

ACKNOWLEDGMENTS

There are so many people in my life that I would like to thank for the opportunity to write this book that I even hate to do so, for fear of leaving a person out. First on my list of thanks must be my wife of 24 years, Patricia Clark, D.D.S., M.S.D., who has been a martial arts widow on too many occasions. My children, Jason and Matthew, who have seen their dad leave home for weeks at a time so that I might be able to teach seminars around the world. Without their understanding and support I would never have been able to pursue the martial arts in the way that I have.

Without a doubt I must thank all of the instructors I have studied under, even if it was only for a day in a seminar—even the white belts I have taught, because they have been able to teach me many lessons in the martial arts. To all of these individuals I owe a deep debt of gratitude. But in the production of this book there were a few people who suffered the photo sessions with good grace and patience. For them there is a special thanks for their effort. They are Shane Leib, Mike Muarry, Steven Webster, Sigbjorn Strommen, Ricco Blom, Patrick Melkersson, Mikael Ogren, and I would also like to thank my editor, George Donahue, who has been very helpful with the production of this book, and without whose support this book would never have come to fruition.

Contents

FOREWORD BY JANE HALLANDER

In my fifteen years as a martial arts journalist, I have seldom seen a martial artist with the ability and knowledge of Professor Rick Clark. Professor Clark is a person who not only knows several martial arts from all angles, but can also write about them in a manner everyone easily understands. From the basic to the most advanced fighting techniques, Professor Clark explains and demonstrates them clearly and with the knowledge of someone who can perform those techniques as second nature. His book is a treasure for levels starting with beginning martial artists, up to the most advanced. Not only does he detail important theories and martial arts principles, but he also delves into rare, little-known techniques and fighting applications. This is a book for all martial arts styles, not limited to a small segment of the martial arts world—as are most books. It is a must read for students, teachers, and those interested in learning more about common-sense martial arts and self defense.

Author and photojournalist Jane Hallander has written for *Black Belt*, *Inside Kung-Fu*, *Martial Arts Training*, *Karate International*, *Inside Karate*, *Inside Tae Kwon Do*, *Tae Kwon Do Times*, *Dojang*, *Dojo*, and *Kung Fu* magazines.

FOREWORD BY VINCE MORRIS

In the world of the martial arts, there is much that is dross, much that is flim flam, and much that is simply bogus.

In this world, there are happily a few teachers who stand out from the morass and whose work illuminates much of the darkness.

As someone whose background was firmly seated in Japanese instruction and who followed a similar course of discovery, I can appreciate perhaps more than most the qualities of resolution and determination that were necessary to overcome the blinkered and short-sighted attitudes of so many who should have known better in bringing the truths of the martial arts into focus.

I have a saying: "You can tell the quality of a teacher by the quality of his students!"

Having had the privilege of working with a number of Sensei Clark's students I can say quite honestly that they are a credit not only to his knowledge, but also to his methods of teaching, which are both effective and inspirational. That is to say, he not only enlarges their technical knowledge, but also instills within them the passion to learn more and then to understand the principles beneath the surface knowledge. Thus a student who has Sensei Clark as his master will be encouraged to seek out the truth and will not be confined to the narrow reaches of any particular style or method.

Given the prevalent protectionist attitude of many of today's teachers, this brings us immediately back to the example of the true Okinawan masters, who would encourage their students to achieve mastery by learning from others.

Master Clark has a broad, eclectic depth of knowledge upon which he has based his teaching, and from which he has teased out those areas of common ground that underlie all true martial arts and that are often neglected in the present day aim of sporting success and the collection of medals.

The student who carefully applies the methods he or she receives from this teacher will be able to have the confidence that the techniques will be effective in the real world, where the only worthwhile trophy is to go home with a safe skin.

The understanding that he or she will gain will also serve to shed light on a vast range of techniques, because the principles themselves will be clear.

I wish master Clark well, and I hope he will continue to tread his path so that he can continue to exemplify the concept embodied within the word "Sensei"—one who has trodden the path before and who now guides others along it!

—Vince Morris (BA Hons.) 6th Dan
Chief Instructor Kissaki-Kai Karate-Do
Director International Institute for Kyusho-Jutsu Research
American Society for Law Enforcement Trainers

PREFACE

As many have stated previously, martial arts is a lifelong pursuit. In 1962 when I first began my training, I was 14 years old. I was young, flexible, in good physical shape; now, in 2000, I am 51 years old, not as young, not as flexible, and not in the best of shape. But I am confident I am a better martial artist today than 37 years ago. I am a better martial artist today than I was 20 years ago, or 10 years ago. Each day should be viewed as an opportunity to become a better person and martial artist. I hope that in the remaining years of my life I will continue to develop as a martial artist and as a human being.

One very strong influence on my martial arts was my first instructor, Wesley Hughes. He was in a very bad car accident and unfortunately was confined to a wheelchair as a quadriplegic. While this might have caused a lesser man to give up the martial arts, he continued to coach our club from his wheelchair. There have been times I have not felt like teaching a class or working out because of a headache, cold, or other malady. But how could I let a little thing like that stop me when Hughes Sensei would not stop? What kind of a lesson did that teach me? I don't think I would be able to adequately express my feelings even in a book. I hope you will be able to glean some small measure of my gratitude and respect for my first instructor.

The gratitude I have is not just to my first instructor, but to each and every instructor I have had the privilege of learning from. Some did not even know they were teachers of mine; for you see, I have learned valuable lessons from tenth-kyu students as well as tenth-dan. Some lessons have been learned outside of the dojo in other fields of endeavor, and others from brief interactions. You must be prepared to learn and apply knowledge from any source and be grateful you were able to understand the lesson.

Knowledge is important in two respects: the benefit you will derive and the benefit of your experience to those you teach. If you have ever practiced any sport and attempted to pass on your knowledge, you may have thought of this at some point. What we know today is not what we will know tomorrow.

Our present base of knowledge forms the building blocks upon which we can strengthen and increase our ideas and knowledge, which change as we mature in our art. So what I put on paper today is not what I would write 10 or 20 years from now. But, I don't have the luxury of waiting those years to pass on what little knowledge I will accumulate over the years. Nor will I be able to put down in these few pages all that I have been taught and all that I have synthesized in the past 37 years. So I must be content with the final draft of this book, being aware that any and all of my presently held convictions and beliefs could be changed the day after I send the manuscript away to my editor, George Donahue. I must be content in the fact that I have the ability to continue to write and will do so.

Another simple point I would like to make is that you will not find anything in this book that you would not be able to find written by others—but perhaps the way I have put the information from various sources together is somewhat different. Sometimes a different way of looking at or hearing something strikes a chord, and you understand a point someone else has been trying to get across to you for quite some time. Perhaps it's nothing more than seeing that another person is in the same situation as you that makes an impact.

Any system of martial arts can benefit from the use of vital points in conjunction with normal training. Vital points offer several major advantages to the individual.

1. Techniques that use vital points require less power in delivery to effectively defend oneself. These points can be used in combination with simple self-defense techniques commonly taught in martial arts classes and well known to martial artists.

2. Vital-point techniques can be extremely effective in self-defense. Smaller or younger individuals can effectively apply these points to stronger, larger, or older individuals—a distinct advantage in a self-defense situation. If they were to rely strictly on strength, the disparity between the individuals could provide a gap too large to close. However, the use of vital points does offer a bridge to cover this

gap. Skill in applying the technique, as always, is the only limiting factor. A few years back, I was teaching a self-defense class; on the first day of class I covered a few simple techniques. Later that evening, one of my students was assaulted in precisely the manner covered in class earlier that day. The student responded with one of the techniques taught and, to her surprise, found her assailant on the ground in pain. She was able to get to her car and escape the scene of her assault. There were three very surprised individuals in this incident. Her assailant, I'm sure, was quite surprised that the small woman put him on the ground in pain in a matter of seconds. My student must have been equally startled at the successful application of the techniques. I was the third person surprised by her ability to recall and utilize the techniques taught only hours before. I can't remember any situation in which a student with only one lesson had been assaulted after class and was able to defend herself using the techniques just taught.

3. Vital points used in conjunction with traditional martial arts offer a major advantage to students and instructors by allowing a variable response. You can increase or decrease the level of force used in accordance with the situation presented. This is extremely important in the area of corrections and law enforcement because of the concern over excessive use of force. As private citizens we can also be held responsible for the use of excessive force when defending ourselves from aggression.

    In corrections and law enforcement, one of the primary guidelines with regard to the use of force is that you can use only the force necessary to secure compliance with your lawful orders. Once compliance is achieved, the use of force beyond that point is unlawful. When we as civilians are forced to defend ourselves, we face the same guidelines. While the law will vary from state to state and country to country concerning the use of force in defending yourself, I feel confident in stating that in any jurisdiction if you use force greater than needed to deter the attack or to defend yourself, there may be sanctions leveled against you. It is imperative that we as instructors and students of the martial arts have a variety of responses to situations available. This is one of the major advantages I feel that the use of vital points offers.

When we look at *bunkai* (analysis of a movement's applications), there are at least seven levels of responses to be found in the various kata. They are:

1. Blocking

2. Numbing or localized pain due to vital point strikes

3. Joint manipulation to cause pain, compliance, dislocation, or breaking

4. Throwing techniques

5. Grappling techniques

6. Knocking out your opponent

7. Potentially fatal techniques.

These responses offer martial artists various levels of response to fit the various situations that they may face.

Bunkai involving blocking is comparatively standard in most systems. When you use blocking techniques, your opponent has no compelling reason to discontinue further attacks. In fact when you simply block an oncoming attack, you have merely postponed the inevitable second attack. If you watch boxing on television, you'll notice that the punches of the boxers are either blocked or slipped. Both competitors can continue the match, provided the punches do not cause enough damage for the fight to be declared a TKO, or for one individual to be knocked down for the count of 10.

When you can strike an arm or a leg in such a manner as to numb that limb, or create an intense amount of pain, you have stepped up your responses in the use of force continuum. In many situations this may be all that is necessary to deter further attack or allow you to escape. If you can numb the leg of your attacker he may find that his ability to stand is greatly impeded. Likewise, if his arm is numbed to the point that he is unable to grab or punch, you have dramatically reduced his ability to successfully complete an attack on your person.

You may find yourself in a situation that is violent enough that you must cause your opponent a more serious injury. When you break or dislocate an attacker's joint, the ability of that individual to use that body part in a continuation of the attack is degraded. Even if you break a bone or dislocate a joint, some individuals may not be impeded in their assault on your person. If an individual is under the influence of certain drugs, his tolerance to pain is greatly increased. "Angel dust" is one of the illegal drugs that give individuals a high degree of tolerance to pain and make it more difficult for police officers to arrest them. If you are faced with an attacker who does not respond to pain or to a joint being broken, it is possible that the individual is under the influence of some type of drug.

Knocking your opponent out with vital-point technique can be a very humane way of defending yourself. Knockouts do not necessarily cause a joint or bone to be broken or even a bruise to occur. It is possible in controlled situations such as seminars or in the dojo for qualified instructors to demonstrate and teach knockouts. When done in this way, knockouts seem to pose little or no threat to the student. In all of the seminars I have taught around the world and in those that my students have taught, I have never heard of one incident where there has been any injury from such techniques. This assumes that due care and caution are being taken by the instructor, and that the instructor is knowledgeable in this aspect of the martial arts. In unskilled or untrained hands, such techniques could be very dangerous. So it is imperative that due caution be exercised in the performance of these techniques. The reason I feel that a knockout may be considered a humane method of self-defense is that in many instances these techniques can be performed with little or no adverse reaction. This is substantially different from typical martial arts techniques. For example, percussive arts strikes to the face could result in a broken nose, teeth being avulsed, or a jaw being broken. Strikes or kicks to the body could result in broken ribs or ruptured organs. Throws, joint locks, and chokes, when used outside the sporting context, offer equally traumatic results. However, vital points offer variable responses to aggression and, as a result, the effect could prove to be more humane.

The last and obviously most devastating result would be to cause the demise of an individual from any martial arts technique. Many vital-point charts list points that are reputed to be fatal. Thankfully I cannot verify from personal experience that any of these vital points are deadly. It appears from review of the standard martial arts texts that the various charts, and stated results, offer a high degree of consistency. Some of the texts I've reviewed appear to have exactly the same charts and diagrams of the body.

As a note of caution, any time that you strike vital points, the safety of your training partner should be paramount. If you are unsure of the results of such strikes, it is better to push the points and ascertain the effects. It is possible to increase the amount of pressure or to lightly tap a particular point to determine its effectiveness. Caution must be exercised, in that some vital points are so sensitive that you could cause a knockout with a single finger. If you were to strike these points properly, just imagine the effect of such a technique. I cannot over-emphasize the potential hazards of striking vital points without proper supervision or guidance.

The range of responses available to meet various levels of threat is one of the major advantages of the utilization of vital points. This clearly fits into the use of force continuum utilized by law-enforcement and correction personnel. Civilians can make use of this concept as well, giving them an appropriate response level. No one wishes to use excessive force in self-defense. Not only would this be unethical, but it would leave you vulnerable to prosecution. It would be tragic to use excessive force defending yourself from an assault and end up serving a prison sentence.

CORE
PRINCIPLES

Do not think always in one straight line.

— Hozoin School (1600 A.D.)

In this chapter I would like to look at what I consider to be some of the core principles of the martial arts I teach. These core principles can offer you some alternate constructs when analyzing various aspects of the martial arts. In addition, some of these concepts may prove useful in other situations in your life. For example, "out-of-the-box thinking," "fault-tolerant systems," "Ockham's Razor," and "Pareto's 80-20 Law" are concepts found in the business world and philosophy, yet they offer us some insights into the martial arts.

These core principles are not written in stone; they offer some alternate ways of looking at a problem and perhaps a solution not otherwise apparent. Principles can be added to this list at any time, and you may have some principles you feel should be added to this short list. As I become aware of other concepts that offer insight into my teaching and training, I will gladly add them to my core principles. We should always endeavor to increase the body of knowledge and our understanding of the martial arts. I have often found it interesting to discover principles in the strangest places; you could be reading a book on philosophy or business and find a principle that relates to the martial arts. Read and expand your knowledge, not only in the area of martial arts but in other areas as well.

The following concepts are touched on briefly, but entire chapters and books could be written on any one of these concepts. This is beyond the scope of this text and my limits as well. So, let's get to it!

Integration of Techniques

In martial arts training we tend to specialize in a particular style. Broadly speaking, these styles could be classified according to the types of techniques predominantly used in the system. Karate, tae kwon do, kung fu, and other such arts tend to center techniques on the percussive arts, such as punching and kicking. Arts such as judo, jujitsu, and aikido base their arts on throws, joint locking, strangulation, and grappling techniques. Within each of these arts there are preferred ranges from which practitioners choose to perform their techniques. As an example, you expect a judo-ka to prefer a close range with a potential aggressor. Individuals who practice the percussive arts would tend to prefer a greater distance between themselves and their aggressor. Even within major categories of systems you'll notice a difference in preferred range for techniques. Generally speaking, tae kwon do is considered to be a longer-range system then various Okinawan systems. The same can hold true for the various arts that are similar to judo and jujitsu.

Lateral Thinking/Critical Thinking

When looking into various martial arts techniques, it is extremely important that we be able to critically analyze anything that is presented to us by our instructors. There are times that explanations for techniques do not make sense, yet we accept them without giving conscious thought to the explanation. If we were to take these ideas and bring them to the light of day, close scrutiny might reveal glaring holes. As an example, there are various stretching techniques that are commonly taught in the dojo because that is the way the instructor was taught. From current research in the field of physical education, we find that ballistic stretching can be dangerous to the students. Yet this type of technique is still commonly taught to the students. The serious instructor should, in my opinion, make use of any current literature that could decrease the use of dangerous techniques, and institute techniques that could improve the performance of his or her students.

As instructors, we should train ourselves to closely observe the techniques within our own system as well as those from other styles. We should be able to observe and analyze to determine when techniques are being performed to the maximum efficiency possible. As part of a critical analysis, we should be able to determine if a technique is effective and if the individual is performing the technique with maximum efficiency. As instructors, this will allow us to give corrective feedback to our students, to increase their performance. We will also be able to absorb useful information on other systems and perhaps integrate it into our primary system.

Take, for example, students who are having trouble with their balance. You could look at the position of their feet or their heads, or how erect they were during the execution of the technique. You might have to observe them performing this technique from several different angles to get a clear view of their problem. The ability to move around and view their technique from all angles gives you a distinct advantage. You are able to observe the students in a way that they cannot do. Of course they could take videotapes of their technique, but feedback would not be instantaneous. Nor would they have the sage advice of their instructor. The ability to step away and see the technique outside of normal situations can provide invaluable feedback.

Many times, individuals see what they expect to see. Try this simple experiment: Read the box below only one time, and at the same time count aloud the Fs in that sentence. Remember, read this only one time, and count them ONLY ONCE—do not go back and count them again. Do not proceed without first reading the small paragraph in the box.

> Finished files are the result of
> years of scientific study combined
> with the experience of years.

If you're like most individuals, you will have found three Fs. If you are quite sharp you may have spotted four or even five. It's highly unusual for anyone to see all six Fs on one read-through. In fact some people even have a hard time spotting all six when they are told the correct number. For some reason we do not spot the Fs and see them as Vs or completely disregard "of."

Once you see how this problem is solved, it becomes quite obvious to you, and you wonder how you could have been so lax in not spotting all six Fs. Bunkai, I think, is very similar to this test. Once you are given certain keys to understanding, it's easy to begin to see various techniques in a different light. You'll be able to look at individual movements found in the kata and draw connections that heretofore you had not made.

OUT-OF-THE-BOX THINKING

To me this is one of the most important concepts I would like you to consider. If you look at your particular martial arts from the same perspective year after year, you may find yourself with tunnel vision.

Trevor Leggett (1993) relates the story of a kendo master who had his students launch attacks on his person anytime or anyplace they felt they might be successful. One time a student felt the master was inattentive and attacked him while he was in the kitchen. As the student attacked with a sword, the instructor grabbed the nearest object at hand to use as a defensive weapon. As luck would have it, there were two large lids for saucepans next to him. The master was able to deflect the sword strikes and subdue the student. The ability of the kendo master to utilize pot lids rather than his sword demonstrated his ability to quickly respond to a situation with an appropriate response. The use of an alternate weapon clearly demonstrates "out-of-the-box thinking" and the mastery of the instructor. However, the student was unable to grasp the full implication of the lesson and mistakenly assumed that saucepan lids could be superior to the sword.

The student, who had misunderstood the point of the lesson, began developing techniques that made use of saucepan lids. From this, a school of martial arts developed from the demonstration of the master. The pupil did not understand that the lids were the nearest item to the master and were utilized for that reason alone. If he had attacked the master later in the day, or the next day, he would have been in a different location and would have made use of what ever item was available. This student became so fixated with the master's demonstration that he failed to see the larger picture. This fixation on the action rather than on the underlying lesson can be a common fault with many a martial artist. If he had been able to utilize "out-of-the-box thinking," he would have seen what the true lesson of the master was: once the technical skill has been achieved with the sword, being able to then improvise a defensive tactic with objects at hand (p. 72).

If you practice percussive arts such as karate or tae kwon do, you tend to concentrate on punching and kicking techniques. It has been my experience that many students and instructors of these techniques are somewhat uncomfortable with joint-locking techniques, throwing, and break falls. Those who practice judo and jujitsu often seem to have difficulty with punching and kicking techniques. This is not to say that individuals in each of these arts cannot be competent in techniques found in other arts, only that we tend to focus on our particular style or system. This seems to be a result of the modern era, when martial arts are taught as budo rather than *bujutsu*. In bujutsu you would have learned a more complete system of martial arts, as they were designed to be used in the battlefield. A warrior would have had to be skilled in the use of weapons, percussive techniques, joint locks, throws, and grappling techniques. Just like any member of our current military, the warriors of the past would have been well versed in any and all of the methods of waging war. Because their lives were on the line, it is only sensible to believe they would have made use of the most effective means at hand. Technology and skill would have had the same advantage several hundred years ago as they do today. Hokama relates how under the Satsuma, the invasion of Okinawa in 1609 lasted only two weeks. The deciding factor in these battles was the use of firearms in the possession of the Japanese. From that point on, the Japanese enforced a ban on weapons and restricted the use of iron to government-appointed blacksmiths. Any iron used in the production of items not used as weapons was imported, because Okinawa did not produce iron. The distribution and use of iron were strictly controlled by the occupying forces. Now just as then, firearms offer a tactical advantage over edged weapons, and even more so against empty hands. No one in full possession of his or her faculties would willingly use an inferior weapon for defense against a superior one. So today, as in the past, we do not necessarily rely on martial arts as our primary method of self-defense. Although our times are violent, as individuals we're not exposed to the same dangerous conditions individuals may have faced 500 years ago. Today we have modern police forces that can respond quickly in our time of need. This is not to say we must abrogate our personal responsibility for all our safety. In fact I would argue that we should prepare ourselves as best we can to defend ourselves against aggression.

The modern budo forms were not designed to give individuals a complete form of self-defense. They were designed to promote physical and mental well-being, as well as offer moral guidelines for individuals. It is equally true that all elements of effective self-defense were not stripped away and can still be found in the kata. When we look at traditional kata, it is important to remember that these forms may be several hundred years old. They were designed with real fighting applications in mind. Individuals would practice these kata to maintain their ability to defend themselves. Kata at that time was not done to win a trophy in a tournament. For these masters of the martial arts, kata and bunkai were deadly serious. These warriors had competence in all of the combative arts. They would have been skilled in throwing, joint locks, strangulation, weapons, and percussive arts. Today, if we're skilled only in the percussive techniques of the martial arts we will not be able to visualize bunkai that involve joint locks, throws, or grappling. To be able to see these techniques in the various kata, an individual must have a strong working knowledge of techniques outside of his or her core system. Remember that in the old days the martial artists would have had a well-rounded background in various methods of unarmed and armed combat. So, as a modern practitioner, gaining a better understanding of your kata requires you to become familiar with other systems and their techniques.

We're lucky in that we have access to a great number of books, videotapes, and instructors to increase our knowledge. Another advantage we have in modern times is the opportunity to train with a number of highly skilled martial artists in seminar settings. These advantages we possess should not be squandered. Serious martial artists should develop a professional library. Standard texts on various martial arts should be acquired and studied. Videotapes are available featuring many of the senior martial artists of our day, and it is possible to find video footage of many martial artists who are no longer living. With our ability to obtain and view this footage, we can in some small sense learn from their teaching. Seminars are a very interesting way we can broaden our knowledge of the martial arts. Not only do you get the opportunity to receive instruction from some very skilled instructors, but you will also have the ability to interact and train with other instructors who are attending the seminar. We tend to place the masters of old in positions of great respect, as well we should. But it is also important to remember that in the future, the masters of today may be seen in the same light in which we view our masters of old.

As our skill in the martial arts increases, we will have a better understanding of bunkai. It is critical that we develop martial skills outside of our core system to have a clear view of bunkai. Obviously, martial artists of yore were skilled in multiple disciplines. It may not be practical for the modern practitioner to devote a substantial amount of time to the practice of other arts. It is possible, however, to obtain books and videos, and attend seminars to increase our knowledge. Once we are able to gain this experience, we should be able to relate our new learning experience to our existing bodies of knowledge. We may then gradually extend our concepts, knowledge, and skills rather than start from ground zero. This is particularly true if we're looking at systems that present overlapping concepts. Take for example karate and tae kwon do; both systems make use of punching and kicking techniques that are very similar. In fact, modern tae kwon do finds its roots in Shotokan karate. The kata of the early systems in Korea were basically the same forms as are found in Shotokan. Later, due to nationalist pride, the forms of tae kwon do were changed to give a more Korean "feel" to the systems. Getting past the basic differences in terminology and preferences for various techniques, the systems are remarkably similar. If an individual has studied karate or tae kwon do for a period of time, it is relatively simple for him or her to learn the other style. Judo, jujitsu, and aikido share many similar features. It is not difficult to cross-train in these arts. It is more difficult for a martial artist who has trained exclusively in karate or tae kwon do to participate in a grappling-based art.

Elements that are common to similar systems tend to be more numerous than those elements that are completely different. When you look across systems, it is important to look at similar concepts within the systems. These key skills in the arts should be developed in the repertoire of instructors. The ability to learn and teach concepts should be considered a crucial skill for us. Martial arts has a complex body of knowledge that can be divided into various subsets of skill and knowledge. At the basic level of instruction, various arts will emphasize particular subsets of knowledge. For example, in grappling arts one of the basic subsets of knowledge is skills in breakfall techniques. This same category of techniques can be found in the percussive arts and would probably be taught later in the curriculum. Similarly, a basic subset of skills in the percussive arts is the punching and kicking techniques. These techniques would probably appear later in the curriculum of the grappling arts. Aikido would probably place the skills in punching as a very low priority, and kicking techniques have even a lower priority in this system. Each system will evidence techniques for which it has a preference. This may simply be a matter of the preference of the founder of the system, or culture may play an important role.

It must be clear by now that I consider the ability to isolate, analyze, and utilize key concepts to be an important skill. You do not expect beginning students of the martial arts to have sufficient skill for this type of evaluation and utilization of key concepts. In fact, I would suspect that a majority of instructors give little thought to the various core concepts of their art. Any discussion of theoretical principles would probably occur in a social setting rather than the dojo. This is not to say that theoretical discussions of individual techniques are absent from the dojo, but it seems likely that skills would be the main order of the day. If you can discover the core principles of your art, then it is a small step to analyzing the core principles of other arts. Thus, if you wish to cross-train, your time could be well spent on the foundation techniques of an art rather than on the techniques requiring higher skill.

Once you have developed complex capabilities in a particular art and have developed foundation skills in other arts over time, you should be able to gradually increase your abilities. Higher skill levels in multiple arts require a smooth integration of techniques. This increase in skill will allow you to integrate discrete techniques into a unitary complex whole.

Black belts will have a vast repertoire of skills in their particular art. Punching, kicking, striking, throwing, grappling, choking, and other skills will be part of their knowledge. It is important for black belts to be able to remember the first day they walked into the dojo. Their skills in the martial arts were zero. The techniques that they now consider to be basic were, at one point in time, extremely complex for them.

It is important for us to develop in our students and ourselves solid foundation skills. These foundation skills can be honed and practiced over an extended period of time until they become habitual. These habitual movements become part of what some call muscle memory. Kata allows us to repetitively practice techniques until the movements our bodies make become second nature. It is at this point that the introduction of bunkai can be critical to the development of self-defense skills.

Avoid Techniques That Require Superior Strength

In the practice of martial arts, many times individuals come to the dojo to learn to defend themselves. They may be small, not have great physical strength, be young or old, male or female. No matter how they present themselves, you must give them techniques that they can use against larger, stronger, younger, older, or more fit opponents. It would seem to be counterproductive to rely on techniques requiring superior strength or agility. We need to be able to teach techniques that will equalize potential disadvantages.

This is one of the major advantages of the use of vital points in conjunction with your core martial arts system. When you attempt to execute a throw, joint lock, or some type of submission hold, size and strength can play a major role in its effectiveness. If prior to applying the technique you are able to strike or press a vital point, you can cause your opponent to lose the use of his limbs or consciousness. It would seem self-evident how valuable this would be in a self-defense situation. Once you have been able to incorporate vital points into your particular martial art, you will be surprised how effective their addition will be.

RELY ON FOUNDATION TECHNIQUES

Techniques for individuals need to be based on simple and reliable movements. In most cases these can be considered to be the foundation techniques of the system. The foundation techniques of a system will be used as the building blocks of all advanced techniques. An example of a foundation technique is a "front kick." This basic kicking technique can be delivered in literally thousands of ways. Yet, without a solid foundation, it would be difficult to deliver the kick in an efficient manner in various circumstances. This holds true for every punch, kick, or strike in the percussive arts. Arts such as jujitsu also have their foundation techniques and require the same amount of attention to detail to build on these solid techniques. An example would be *O Goshi* (major hip throw). Without developing skill in this throw other *koshi-waza* (hip techniques) would be difficult to learn and master.

All percussive systems, whether they are of Okinawan, Japanese, Korean, or Chinese derivation teach similar punching, striking, and kicking techniques. Each system will have particular groups of techniques that they favor, yet all will contain many of the same basic movements. No matter which martial art you practice, there will be always be core techniques that will provide a basic working knowledge of that system. As you begin to cross-train, it is important to learn the basics of other arts. This will offer you a firm base on which to build a more complete system.

KATA-CENTERED PRACTICE

In years past, we did not have available to us the mass distribution of books, videotapes, and magazines. Several hundred years ago martial arts books were copied by hand, a labor-intensive work subject to errors. Today, virtually every city offers some type of self-defense training. There may be various locations that do not have martial arts schools directly in their city, but I suspect with the minimum amount of travel a judo, karate, tae kwon do, aikido, tai chi chuan, or other martial arts school could be found. The availability of information on various martial arts and the number of martial arts schools has dramatically increased in the modern era. Centuries ago information on styles was passed from master to pupil. It was an oral tradition that may or may not have had written documentation. In that time period, literacy was probably restricted to the nobility and/or the merchant classes. Many in the warrior class perhaps were somewhat, or even completely, illiterate. But that is not a given; education clearly was not what we have today. Therefore, instructors would embed information on their particular fighting system within the kata, not only for their own benefit, but for that of their students. Students, as they gained the trust of their master, would be initiated into the secrets of his system. I am firmly convinced that in the modern era, with its emphasis on sports, the more serious applications have fallen into disuse. There has been a minor resurgence in techniques that are more self-defense-oriented.

FAULT-TOLERANT SYSTEM/REDUNDANCY IN TECHNIQUES/ FLEXIBILITY IN TECHNIQUES

Each time you practice techniques with an opponent, you find it is extremely difficult to execute each and every technique perfectly. There are slight variations in your execution of the technique and your opponent's reaction to your movements. They may try to defend themselves in ways that you would not expect. Or they may vary their defense against your techniques. It's sort of like "Murphy's law," if anything can go wrong, it will go wrong. So we have to have techniques that allow for this variation in the movements of your opponent. We need to build redundancy into the techniques to provide a measure of safety to us when, or if, we are ever forced to rely on our martial arts training. All of the techniques need to allow us some degree of error or fault. We cannot take into account every situation that might arise, but we can look at common responses to the various techniques. Hopefully, we can build techniques that are fault tolerant and allow for some margin of error. Kata does take this into account by the use of multiple attacks or continuation of attacks to your opponent. While it is nice to think in terms of "one strike one kill," the reality of self-defense is that we may be forced to use multiple techniques to achieve our goal.

TARGETS OF OPPORTUNITY

When we look at all the points on an acupuncture chart, we have to cull the points that would not be readily accessible during a physical confrontation. Further, we can select points that are known to produce particular responses in our attacker. Over the centuries various points have been categorized as to the result of strikes to them. Results can vary from breaking of a joint, dislocation, ripping of tendons, temporary paralysis, knockouts, or even death. Various schools or systems have detailed various points. It behooves us to study and categorize these points. When you become intimately knowledgeable in the results from such strikes, you will have made tremendous progress in the study of vital points. This information allows you, with some degree of accuracy, to predict the movement of an individual once you have struck him on a vital point. If a person wishes to attack you it will have to be by reaching out with an arm or a leg to cause some type of physical damage. It is true that an individual can stand back a hundred yards or more and shoot you with a gun. However, in this book I am addressing close-quarter combat that may involve punching and kicking techniques or attacks delivered with a handheld weapon. There is a basic assumption that the individual who is attacking you is in close physical proximity to you. Martial arts techniques based on the percussive and grappling arts require you to be able to reach out and make contact with the head, neck area, extremities, or body of your opponent. Once you and your opponent are within the delivery range of your techniques, it is imperative to be familiar with the various vital points. This gives you a choice of targets to attack, or to use another term, "targets of opportunity." In other words, why attack general areas of the body when you can narrow your attacks to specific points or areas and have predictive results of your attacks? Vital points do assure you of a higher degree of successful results of particular attacks.

OCKHAM'S RAZOR

William of Ockham (ca. 1286–1347) was theologian and logician. One of the tools that he's given credit for is the principle of parsimony, commonly known as Ockham's Razor. There are many variations of this rule, but the following has been ascribed to him in one form or another:

(A.) It is futile to do with more what can be done with less.

"Frustra fit per plura quod potest fieri per pauciora."

Never multiply explanations or make them more complicated than necessary. An explanation should be as simple and direct as possible. It is vain to do with more what can be done with less.

(B.) The proposition comes out true for things, if two things suffice for its truth; it is superfluous to assume a third.

"Quando propositio verificatur pro rebus, si duae rei sufficiunt ad eius veritatem, superfluum est ponere tertiam."

(C.) Plurality should not be assumed without necessity.

"Pluralitas non est ponenda sine necessitate."

Entities shall not be multiplied beyond necessity.

(D.) No plurality should be assumed unless it can be proved (a) by reason or (b) by experience or (c) by some infallible authority.

"Nulla pluralitas est ponenda nisi per rationem vel experientiam vel auctoritatem illius, qui non potest falli nec errare, potest convinci."

I suspect part of the reason the term "razor" is used with this principle of Ockham is that you are able to "cut through cleanly" and get to the heart of a complex problem. In many respects this reminds me of the K.I.S.S. principle (keep it simple stupid). There are several schools of thought on why vital-point techniques work and how to predict the outcome of various strikes to vital points. One school of thought feels that all the techniques can be explained in terms of Western medical science. The other school ascribes their explanations to the field of traditional Chinese medicine. Both schools make excellent arguments as to why their paradigm is the correct way to look at vital-point techniques. Both schools can back their claims with a surprising amount of scholarly research. From my perspective, I look to both schools of thought to help provide lucid explanations for vital-point techniques. I do feel that getting too involved in any one theoretical approach can bog down your training. In other words "it's vain to do with more what can be done with less." I tend not to be terribly concerned with the technical explanation as to why certain reactions occur with your training partner. I am a bit more pragmatic and observe the reactions to various strikes and see if these can be replicated with other individuals. From this I attempt to build a repertoire of techniques based on known reactions to the various vital points.

In addition to the simplification of striking vital points, we can use this metaphor to quickly cut through unrealistic bunkai. When analyzing kata we will be reverse-engineering techniques. We are given traditional kata, yet the creator of this kata is no longer living. At best, we can give an educated guess to various bunkai in the kata. We may not be able to tell with a high degree of certainty what the defensive movements are that the kata may involve. I do believe we can have some confidence in what type of attacks the various kata would be defending against. I strongly believe physical attacks remain constant across generation and culture.

Some believe kata were designed for use by the civilian population against other civilians. The use of unarmed combat would not have been used against well-trained warriors. It is easy to understand this position, a warrior when attacking or defending probably would have used some type of weapon if it were at hand. However, there are times when you will not have a weapon, or your weapon could be broken, or you may have been disarmed. At this point you must respond with or without a weapon or forfeit your life. This is the point at which the unarmed traditions come into play.

I think it is important that we, as students and instructors, think in terms of the ways we would most likely be attacked. If you were to list the techniques that you consider yourself to be most likely to encounter in a real confrontation, your response would probably center around pushes, grabs, head butts, head locks, straight leg kicks, hook punches, and overhead strikes from a weapon.

It would seem logical, if we take to heart our analysis of kata, to center on these types of attacks. If our bunkai for kata is based on the types of attacks we're likely to encounter, it is irrelevant if these techniques were not the intended bunkai of the creator of the particular kata we are analyzing. The important factor here is that we have techniques in the kata we practice to defend against the attacks we suspect we will most likely encounter. It does not matter if the bunkai we use was not at first envisioned by the creator of a kata—just so long as we have workable techniques that will be applicable to our particular needs.

Funakoshi is well known for his precept *ikken kissatsu*, "one fist, one kill"; this would be simplicity itself. When looking at kata it behooves us to look for the simple solution. The application should be safe, quick, and effective.

PARETO'S 80-20 LAW

Over a hundred years ago Vilfredo Pareto discovered a statistical relationship that would manifest itself repeatedly in larger systems—the 80-20 law. For example, in business 80 percent of the profits are produced by 20 percent of the employees. Or, you might say that 80 percent of your profits come from 20 percent of your customer base.

In martial arts, I feel we can make use of Pareto's law. Let's look at judo for an example of this rule. The syllabus of judo, or throwing techniques, is contained in the *Gokyo no Waza*. The *Gokyo no Waza* is made up of five groups of techniques, each containing eight throws. This yields the total of 40 different throwing techniques. In 1920, the Kodokan added 17 new techniques, *Shimmeisho no Waza*, to the syllabus of judo. If you look at contest judo or judo practiced in the dojo, you'll find that most students will use or practice a much smaller number of techniques. An individual will probably have 10 or fewer throws that he or she feels comfortable in using. The individual will use these throws the large majority of the time in practice or contest. However, he or she will have developed skill in the other techniques and will apply them as the opportunity arises. But it seems likely you will be able to apply the 80-20 law here. Likewise, in international competition there are certain techniques and throws that appear more regularly then other techniques. Some competitors are well known for their skill in a particular technique. This is not saying that they do not have a great deal of competency in the use of other techniques in judo, but they find a few techniques that work particularly well for them.

I suspect that if you look at the various movements found in karate, you will find a certain group of techniques that tend to be repeated over and over again. Each system will have a core group of techniques that embody the art. For example in tae kwon do, kicking techniques are preeminent over the use of hands. If we are looking at kicks, there are only three major classifications. They are: (1) front kick, (2) sidekick, and (3) roundhouse kick. There are, of course, other kicks, such as the crescent kick, knee kicks, hook kick, and the "returning wave" kick. Yet these first three kicks tend to make up the basis of many other kicking techniques. By adding jumping, skipping, sliding, turning, and other body movements to these basic kicks, you greatly increase the number of kicks. These three kicks are, in effect, foundation techniques for more difficult skills.

Attacks to the individual, I think, can make use of Pareto's Law. If we think about the most common methods of being attacked, we can narrow them down to the few fundamental approaches. They will be:

1. A grab
2. A push
3. A punch
4. A kick

It seems likely that in the majority of self-defense situations you will be confronted by one or more of these attacks.

If you look at a grab, there are only a few ways that an individual will commonly grab. You have a same-side grab, whereby an opponent grabs your left side with their right hand. Or a cross-hand grab, whereby they grab your right side with their right hand. Or a two-handed grab. If you break this down even further, when they grab you they will probably grab either your wrist, forearm, upper arm, lapel, or throat. Of course there are ways to grab you that will not fit into these categories. You may find yourself being grabbed on the leg or ankle. But in the normal situation I would think this to be somewhat unlikely. In other words, 80 percent of the time you'll probably be grabbed in the aforementioned ways, and 20 percent of the time in some way other than those mentioned above. It would therefore seem prudent to spend 80 percent of your time practicing defensive tactics against techniques you could reasonably expect to occur.

Vital points, I think, are a perfect example of the 80-20 law. Over the years, I've been able to identify a large number of vital points, either through scholarly research or through practical experience. It seems strange that when practicing techniques I tend to choose a particular subgroup of points on a regular basis. This experience tends to verify, in my own mind, the importance of Pareto's Law. Each individual, I think, will have to develop a subgroup of points that they feel comfortable utilizing in their techniques. I think this will be a natural selection as the individual's body of knowledge increases.

Universal Principles

This concept is something that I think some martial artists tend to forget. Shakespeare said "a rose by any other name would smell as sweet." To carry this into the martial arts realm, I think you have to say "a punch by any other name is still a punch." If you happened to have a real fight with a martial artist and had your nose broken from a punch, I think it would be impossible to tell if the punch came from a person who practiced karate, tae kwon do, kung fu, judo, or jujitsu. The same would hold true for any other technique that is utilized by more than one system. I've often felt that if you put a group of five martial artists onstage and asked them to perform a punch, front kick, side kick, or other technique, you would be hard-pressed to differentiate the system or style they practiced. There are only so many ways to inflict damage on the human body. Traditional systems of martial arts have been refined over the years to give you the most effective and practical methods of attack and defense. It is only logical that many of the same techniques would be found cross-culturally and across various systems within national boundaries.

It is not surprising therefore to see similar throwing, joint manipulation, punching, striking, and kicking techniques. It would be surprising to find martial arts that did not use techniques that shared similar theoretical foundations. Remember, the joints of all human beings operate in the same manner. There are certain directions joints do not bend in; after a certain point they will either be dislocated or broken. When you execute a front kick, by definition, every system will use similar techniques. Side kicks and roundhouse kicks are no different. There will be minor stylistic differences in kicking techniques, and there will be differences of application. But the primary intent of the kick is to deliver a forceful attack to some part of your opponent's body with your foot. Punching and striking techniques are the same; an individual attempts to deliver a well-focused and powerful attack with his or her hand.

This is what I'm talking about when I speak of universal principles. I'm not particularly interested in the stylistic nuances of particular systems. I am interested in how these techniques are effectively delivered and if there is a carryover between various arts.

THE PARADIGMS:
MODERN AND TRADITIONAL
CHINESE MEDICINE

A mind is like an umbrella–it is only useful when it's open.

Currently, as we look for explanations of what makes techniques effective, martial artists tend to divide into three major camps. There are those who exclusively make use of information gained in the fields of medicine, physiology, and anatomy. Others make use of traditional Chinese medicine to explain how vital-point techniques work. The third camp, in which I include myself, is eclectic. That is to say we look for explanations from Western medical science and traditional Chinese medicine. Western medical science offers many powerful explanations for us and conforms to our belief in science and technology. However, there are some reactions that appear to defy explanation by Western medical science. Traditional Chinese medicine offers explanations, using an alternative paradigm. Many may feel that the use of traditional Chinese medicine will provide explanations that correspond to the thought processes used by the old masters of the martial arts. This is undoubtedly true, yet I do not feel that the old masters would have excluded any information from any source that would allow them to gain further knowledge of vital points. To be practical, it would seem fair to take knowledge from any possible source and apply it as best meets our needs. To reject any source of information because it does not fit our primary paradigm would seem to be senseless. The science and theology of any civilization is based on the best information they have at a particular moment in time, and we should be no different. Eastern and Western traditions developed alternate methods of explaining natural phenomena. Each looks at the world from a different perspective, and both types of knowledge have proven to be extremely valuable over the years. To discount information from one tradition or the other seems rather foolish. At least at this point in my life I feel it is important to draw as much information as possible from both camps. This allows me, or you, to develop a wide range of explanations. To say that you'll look at vital points only from the perspective of traditional Chinese medicine or only from that of Western medicine seems limiting. I advocate gathering as much information from both camps as possible and merging that information.

Western Medicine and the Martial Arts

Western medical science offers many explanations for various techniques. I would like offer some examples in the following paragraphs.

Baroreceptors play a part in one of the better-known mechanisms for arterial pressure control. Baroreceptors are spray-type nerve endings found in the walls of large systemic arteries. Baroreceptors can be found in the walls of almost every large artery in the thorax and neck region. There are, however, three locations in the body that contain larger numbers of baroreceptors. They are:

1.   The aortic arch
2.   The carotid sinus
3.   The kidneys

If there is an increasing pressure in the walls of the arteries, signals are transmitted to the central nervous system. In turn, signals are sent through the autonomic nervous system to reduce the arterial pressure to normal.

Strikes to the carotid sinus can elicit the baroreceptor reflex. When struck, signals are transmitted from the carotid sinus through Hering's nerve to the glossopharyngeal nerve; they are then transmitted to the tractus solitarius in the medullary area of the brain stem. Secondary signals are then sent that inhibit the vasoconstrictor center and excite the vagal center. This then causes vasodilation throughout the peripheral circulatory system. This is accompanied by a decrease in heart rate and the strength of heart contractions. The effects of this reflex in some individuals can be so strong as to cause fainting from tight collars (Guyton p. 247).

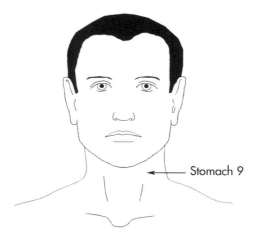

Stomach 9

In a martial context this point (Stomach 9) becomes a very important point. Strikes to this area can knock out your opponent. Strong attacks to this point have the potential to be fatal. This is especially true in individuals who may have plaque buildup in the arteries.

The withdrawal reflex is elicited by the stimulation of pain, which causes a withdrawal from the painful stimuli. For example, if you touch something hot, you pull your hand back rapidly. Or if some part of your body is painfully stimulated, you will pull your body away from that stimulus. If you control an individual's arm and strike Lung 5, his or her opposite hand will be pulled away from you. This reflex is valuable in a self-defense situation. If you're able to accurately strike this point, the withdrawal reflex can cause your opponent's opposite arm to move away from you. Notice in the figure that my partner has turned his body to the side, his left arm is away from me, and his knees have buckled. If you can correctly apply a strike to this point, the likelihood that your opponent will be able to continue with the attack immediately will be greatly diminished. This will give you a split second to continue with your defensive tactics.

Our bodies have various receptors to transmit sensation. There are basically five types of sensory receptors:

1.   Mechanical receptors

2.   Thermal receptors

3   Nociceptors

4.   Electromagnetic receptors

5.   Chemoreceptors

Mechanical receptors detect the deformation of the receptors or the cells next to the receptor. Thermal receptors transmit information on temperature changes. Then nociceptors detect if there has been physical damage or chemical damage to tissue. Electromagnetic receptors respond to light on the retina of our eyes and to light on our skin. The chemoreceptors are responsible for our sense of smell, oxygen levels, carbon dioxide concentrations, and our ability to taste.

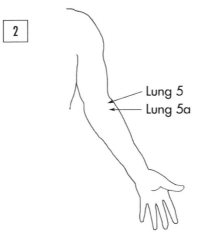

The various sensory receptors, while extremely sensitive to one type of stimulus, are virtually unresponsive to other sensations. In the martial arts, the major classifications of sensory receptors that deserve attention are the mechanical receptors and the nociceptors.

The pacinian corpuscle is a very large sensory receptor. Compression on the pacinian corpuscle deforms and elongates the central core. The pacinian corpuscle is useful in transmitting information about the rapid changes in pressure on the body. It does not give feedback for consistent pressure applied to the body. In other words, this corpuscle transmits information on very rapid pressure applied to tissue; if the pressure is continued, then the excitation diminishes. The pacinian corpuscle is useful in predicting where your body will be in a few seconds. As an example, the pacinian corpuscles located in or around the various joints of the body send information that allows the nervous system to predict where your hands and feet will be next when you're running. This allows the body to make the necessary adjustments to maintain our balance. If we can affect the pacinian corpuscle, we may be able to reduce its predictive function in the body. Some pacinian corpuscles are found in the tissue surrounding the joints. They react very quickly to rapid changes and help determine the rate of rotation of the joint.

Position sense receptors determine the static kinesthetic positions of the body. These receptors can be found in the joint capsules and ligaments, in the receptors of our skin, and in the deep tissue near the joints. The most numerous are the Ruffini endings. The Ruffini endings are of a spray-type and are strongly stimulated when a joint is suddenly moved.

This response could prove useful in grappling situations. For example, if you grab points on the wrist and twist the tissue around the wrist, you can fool the body into feeling that the wrist itself is being rotated. You will notice that it is easy to rotate the arm into position for an arm bar.

The lore of martial arts indicates that there are techniques that will clause death at a later date. In 1247, the *Hsi Yuan Lu* (Instructions to the Coroner) was written by Shun Tzu. This text was translated by Herbert Giles for the *China Review* in 1874. It was republished in 1924 for the *Proceedings of the Royal Society of Medicine*. This text may be the oldest book on forensic medicine ever written. It detailed numerous points that were reputed to cause death either at the moment of impact or at a later time. Recognition that such delays in death could occur, and could be attributed to strikes on vulnerable parts of the body is very interesting. If, for example, you were to strike a point that ruptured the spleen, death would surely occur at a later time if proper medical attention was not received. Internal bleeding would be but one factor in the death. Or, if a distended bladder were struck, it could very well rupture. Urine and blood released in the body cavity would probably cause peritonitis. Deaths in such a manner could give rise to the notion of the "delayed death touch."

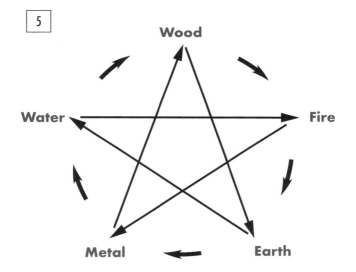

TRADITIONAL ORIENTAL MEDICINE

The oral history of the martial arts tells us that many of the instructors received specialized training in the treatment of traumatic injury. These instructors would teach fighting techniques to students and would be able to serve as caregivers if an injury were to occur during instructional sessions. It is not uncommon during the practice of martial arts for students to get bruises, muscle strains, dislocations, or even breaks. These instructors would have made use of the common modalities of treatment.

At that time, Oriental medicine encompassed a holistic approach to health. Oriental medicine made use of acupuncture and herbal remedies. These systems of treating ailments attempted to balance the internal energy of the body. At its most basic level, Oriental medicine espoused the thought that there are two forces working in the universe, and by extension in the human body. These forces are *Yin* and *Yang* (*In/Yo* in Japanese and *Um/Yang* in Korean). These forces can be seen in the waxing and waning of the moon, male and female, positive and negative; they can be found in every natural phenomenon. By having a balance of these forces within the body good health is assured. If, however, there is an imbalance in the system, poor heath and disease will be inevitable. This balance of the forces of Yin and Yang is not confined to the human body. This model can explain the harmonious functioning of personal relationships, the functioning of the state—virtually every physical or spiritual phenomenon.

In traditional Oriental medicine, this balance of the forces of Yin and Yang can be seen in the various parts of the body as well as in the internal organs. The vital energy of the body travels to various parts of the body via meridians. The meridians have corresponding organs and functions in the body. They also have a relationship with the forces of Yin and Yang. From this the "five elements" concept grew.

In traditional Chinese medicine the world is divided into five elements that interact with each other. In the context of these elements, we see that wood destroys earth, earth destroys water, water destroys fire, fire destroys metal, and metal destroys wood.

When thinking in terms of the various elements, you can use various cues to remember the effects of the cycle. Within the cycle of destruction, wood destroys earth, can be visualized as a tree's roots burrowing into the ground and pushing it to the side. Earth destroys water uses the concept that a glazed clay pot can contain liquids. When water destroys fire is mentioned, you can imagine throwing a bucket of water on a fire to extinguish the flames. Fire destroys metal generates the picture of a forge melting an ingot to a molten mass. Finally metal destroys wood can conjure the image of a saw cutting through a log.

In the cycle of creation Wood is used for fuel to create fire. Fire causes the fuel to become ash, which is seen as Earth. From the earth you would mine metal. If the metal were to melt, its form would appear to be liquid, like Water. The necessary element for the growth of plants and trees is water.

It is important to remember that these elements are metaphors for conceptual ideas. An example is the way the various elements are related to the meridians.

This system, many believe, can be used to develop techniques that will cause the greatest amount of damage to an opponent while using the least amount of physical force. They apply the theory of the five elements to all of the points along a particular meridian. In other words, any point on the Lung meridian would be a metal point. Any point on the Gallbladder meridian would be considered a wood point. According to this line of thought, if you were to strike a Lung point, you would then want to strike a Liver or Gallbladder point to cause maximum damage with minimal force. In other words you would strike a "metal" point, then strike a "wood" point. To give a more concrete example, if you were to strike Lung 5 at a 45-degree angle toward the fingertips, you could then strike Gallbladder 20 with a fist, such as you might do in a rising head block. Be aware that if you do attempt to strike your practice partner you stand a very good chance of knocking him or her out with this combination of strikes. If you are not fully competent in the appropriate *katsu* (revival technique), you should not attempt to knock out your training partner.

One problem with this line of reasoning is that in traditional Chinese medicine the five-elements (phases) concept "plays an important role in point selection only in relation to the Five Transporting (*wu-shu*) points on the extremities" (Kaptchuk p. 355). In other words, the five elements are used in acupuncture only on points from below the elbows to the fingertips and from the knees to the tips of the toes.

The use of the five elements does not play a role in point selection in traditional Chinese acupuncture. However, according to Kaptchuk, "Chinese medicine has had to take many liberties with the Five Phase theory in order to fit it to actual medical experience" (p. 347) so "Five Phases theory does not always agree with this understanding, and in that case, it is simply ignored" (p. 347) . So, from this point of view, it may be possible to ignore the traditional medical applications of the five elements (phases) and apply this theory in a broader sense to attacking the vital points of the body.

Dienes and Flanagan have done ground-breaking research in this aspect of vital points. While their work has not been published, their results have been widely circulated in the martial arts community via the Internet. Zoltan Dienes, Ph.D. is an experimental psychologist at Sussex University and has published at least 32 scientific articles and coauthored a book. He has appeared in British national television and radio shows and newspapers as well as on German nation television discussing his research in the field of psychology. He has been a statistical consultant for several years for two drug companies in the United Kingdom. In addition, he has been practicing Shotokan karate for over 22 years. Mike Flanagan, at the time of their study, was a second-year student (of three) in Shiatsu and is knowledgeable in the field of traditional Chinese medicine (TCM). He has been studying the martial arts for over four years. The combined experience of these two individuals offers a solid basis for researching the role of TCM as it applies to vital points in the martial arts.

In their initial study, they endeavored to test a group with no knowledge of TCM to determine if the use of the five-element theory would increase the reported pain of individuals. The results of their test indicated that there was not a significant difference in the pain rating of a point whether it is was preceded by stimulation of a point as specified by the destructive cycle or as specified by the creative cycle. There were limiting factors in this study, since it was the first, but it did give some interesting results. It does offer some limited validation to the notion that it is not necessary to possess knowledge of TCM theory in order to develop and master vital-point techniques. This study does not undermine TCM in more general terms, only the particular use of the five-element theory as applied to vital points from a martial arts perspective. It is also important to restate that the five-element theory of

Chinese acupuncture was used only on points at or below the elbows and knees. To generalize the five-element theory to other points takes liberties with the theoretical basis of TCM as described by Kaptchuk and others.

Remember, acupuncture is used to cure the individual of illness. The intent of martial artists when they apply pressure point techniques in life and death situations is to kill or seriously injure their opponent. Some of the vital points used in self-defense applications are not even shown on acupuncture charts. The same techniques can also be explained by reference to Western medical science, for the most part. It would be highly unlikely that a physician would be able to give a reasonable explanation for why an individual should be knocked out by striking the arm or leg. It would seem that a combination of both Western physiology and anatomy and Eastern acupuncture theory would offer some of the best explanations.

According to acupuncture theory, there is a definite flow of energy in the human body. The energy starts in the Lung meridian and flows to the large intestine, stomach, spleen, heart, small intestine, bladder, kidney, pericardium, triple warmer, and gallbladder, and ends with the liver. The process is then started again and continually makes this circuit in the body over a twenty-four-hour period. The appendix provides a list of the various meridians of the body, with names for the various points given in Chinese, Korean, and Japanese as well as charts for the various points used in acupuncture. As a caveat, there is a wide variety of ways in which to Romanize foreign words. The most effective way to learn the pronunciation of each of the points would be to have a native speaker teach you the pronunciation of each of the points from the Chinese characters. You may find various books on acupuncture that will give a different spelling of various points; unfortunately this is unavoidable. There may be Romanized names for vital points found in other books that differ greatly from the names used in acupuncture. Names for vital points may have been given different names within a particular style for reasons of secrecy. If a person found a document that listed the various vital points used within that system, it would be useless to him unless he has been initiated into the "secrets" of that style. This list, therefore, should be used with the understanding that it is neither perfect nor complete. Compiling information on vital points is a "work in progress"; as with computers, you must go with the most current technology and upgrade your system when new technology becomes available.

Within acupuncture theory, there are times when the flow of *ki* is at its maximum and other times when the flow is at its weakest (See Figure 1, p. 23). We do know that the body has biological rhythms for its various functions. This may have been observed many centuries ago and developed into the theory of acupuncture. Some who teach and write on the subject of vital-point techniques hold the opinion that you must strike vital points in conjunction with the time of day to achieve the maximum effect. Smith (1974) quotes Master Ho Yu-shan when he states "To speak of spotting in accordance with time periods is deceitful; boxers used this to puzzle people." Spotting in this reference refers to striking vital points of the body. I am of the opinion that striking points according to the times of day may allow you to strike with lighter force to get an effect in a class or seminar situation. In a real-life confrontation, you will not be allowed the luxury of picking vital points to strike. You will be forced by the situation to attack those points that are the closest to you and most open to attack. The theory of the ebb and flow of the energy of the body may hold true for acupuncture; it does not seem necessary for martial arts applications. In acupuncture you are stimulating a point with a very small needle; in the martial arts you are applying much greater stimulation with a strike or kick.

Some instructors feel that there is an important relationship between the seasons, months, or moon phases. While there may be validity to these suggestions in acupuncture, it does not seem to play a critical role in the application of martial arts techniques. For example, it does not seem practical for us to take into consideration what points would be most active or least active in a particular season and then mount a defense using this logic. In the heat of battle, you will react on an instinctive level to your opponent's attack. You do not have the luxury of choice; you must respond without thought. Your success or failure at that moment will be based on sweat, hard work, and practice in the dojo.

One of the main problems I see with total reliance on TCM for predictive value is how all-encompassing TCM can be. It takes little thought to see that every possible combination of points can be achieved by using either the cycle of destruction or the cycle of creation. You can, at random, choose any two points on the acupuncture charts and determine that strikes should cause damage to your opponent. For example if we strike a wood point (liver or gallbladder), the cycle of destruction would tell us that the most effective points to attack next would be earth (stomach or spleen). Or, if we used the cycle of creation, once striking wood points (liver and gallbladder) the next logical strikes would be to the meridians associated with fire (heart and small intestine). It is impossible to select any two points that do not correspond to either the cycle of destruction or the cycle of creation. It's obvious that all combinations of points are included in either the cycle of creation or the cycle destruction. If there are no exclusions, any predictive value of using this theory would appear to be suspect. This is not to say that Chinese medicine does not offer metaphors to describe particular reactions. However, it's use to predict the effects of various strikes seems to be problematic. In addition, you can add in other "laws" of acupuncture to fill in any cracks in logic that may develop. Or you can use these other "laws" to rationalize why a technique works so effectively.

This is not to say there can be no use for acupuncture theory when discussing vital point attacks. One of the major reasons to be familiar with the points used in acupuncture is the ability to pass on information to others using the notation of TCM. This in and of itself is a major reason to become familiar with the various points used in acupuncture.

When you practice any martial art that incorporates vital points, it will be important to remember that these techniques were designed to cause serious injury to your opponent. There are revival techniques that are taught to senior students. Different instructors will have various criteria for teaching these techniques to students. In my personal opinion, teaching revival techniques can pose a more serious issue than teaching the vital points in your class. In classes that do not emphasize vital-point techniques, there are dangerous and potentially deadly effects from the standard repertoire of techniques. When you add the potential for knocking out your opponent with a light strike to various parts of the body, you increase your obligation as an instructor to choose appropriately the methods you use to disseminate information. If students are taught methods of resuscitation, they may have the mistaken belief that they are expert in all areas of vital points. They may attempt potentially dangerous techniques with their training partner, not considering the potential effects of their technique. Therefore, I make it a practice to teach only those instructors I personally know and trust revival techniques for knockouts.

This is analogous to a firearms instructor who teaches members of the military how to effectively use firearms. The soldiers' intent and purpose is not to wound or disable, it is to kill the enemy. If, in the course of war, they wound an enemy soldier, they have not been taught how to remove the bullets and save the life of that individual. Others are trained to do that. The foot soldiers' job is to kill their enemy. While I do not believe it is the job of an individual in a self-defense situation to kill the person who is attacking him or her, I do feel that they have the right to use the necessary force to forestall further aggression. If in the course of your legitimate reaction to unwarranted aggression the other individual is injured and requires medical attention, it is the responsibility of trained medical personnel.

Striking vital points with the intent and purpose of causing serious injury or damage to an individual could result in that person's death. It is equally true that you may knock out that individual, and various bodily functions may be arrested. Hancock (1904) notes "Among Occidental readers there is a notion that, because one who has been killed by a fatal blow can be brought back to life, he was not really killed after all. When a fatal jiu-jitsu [*sic*] blow is struck in the right way the processes of life are mechanically stopped. It requires the prompt manipulations of *kuatsu* [*sic*] to set these vital forces at work again by mechanical means, and thus to restore life."

While many of the vital points used are related to acupuncture points, a considerable number are not. It is possible to strike what you think is a single acupuncture point, but in reality you may be striking one or more vital points not recognized in acupuncture. Acupuncture points are used to restore the vital energy in a person, and thus to restore their health. It is important to recognize the fact that vital points used in the martial arts are designed to destroy or disrupt the flow of energy in the body. Acupuncture makes use of similar points to restore the chi, so that there is a healing of the individual. When a skillful acupuncturist stimulates these points by massage, moxabustion, or needling, they will affect a specific meridian, with a positive result. Yet, if this same point is struck, using various angles or directions of attacks, it could affect a totally different meridian, with very serious consequences. Advanced practitioners of vital-point attacks will have acquired the ability to affect at least three different meridians. They, will also have learned to control other effects with their strikes so as to delay the effects of their attack. Without question, it is important that all practice of pressure point techniques be performed under the strict supervision of a qualified instructor. The instructor will have received training on how to recognize that each technique affects the vital forces of the body. Additionally, they will be able to correct or alleviate any harmful effects from such practice.

It would be well to heed some sound advice from almost 100 years ago: "Never more than indicate the fatal blows unless there be an expert at Kautsu [sic] [revival techniques] at hand!" If you do not follow these basic rules you will find, at the very least, that your partner will exhibit side effects. These could include nausea, diarrhea, headaches, excessive soreness, numbness, fainting, or even more severe symptoms. This could occur immediately after strikes to pressure points or up to two weeks after your practice session. It is more likely, however, that these symptoms will occur in a matter of hours after the practice session.

As with any general guidelines, there are exceptions to the rule. There are places on the body where there is a convergence of vital points in a small area, which will allow two, three, four, or even five vital points to be struck at the same time. The points where three or more vital points can be struck at one time can cause an instantaneous knock out or even death. To underscore this problem, many of the vital points used by martial artists are related to acupuncture points, while others are not. There are quite a few important vital points that are not listed on acupuncture charts.

When working with these vital points from the perspective of traditional Chinese medicine, you are manipulating the vital energy of your partner. By manipulating the energy flow you can cause very serious results in your opponent, which can run the full range from pain to death. There are three basic ways in which you manipulate the energy flow of your training partner:

1. You can back up the energy flow so that it returns to the source of the energy. An analogy for this would be plugging a normal household radio into a 220-volt line. The energy would cause the radio to malfunction, to say the least.

2. Or you can pull energy away from the source to cause a disruption. This would be similar to having multiple appliances plugged into a single circuit breaker. If the energy consumption is too great, the circuit will blow.

3. The final way is to block the energy from entering into an area of the body. This would be similar placing a dam over a small stream. The water is cut off. And soon the level of water is cut down to a trickle. An example of this is pressing into the wrist pressure point on the ulnar side of the arm, which allows you to bend the wrist.

When you are manipulating pressure points, you will find that there are no pressure points that can be attacked in a straight motion. All pressure points must be attacked at an angle. In most cases, you will attack pressure points at a 45-degree angle. This is one of the reasons why the traditional "full twist" punch is not as effective as the technique advocated in this book.

As you practice vital points, you will discover that there are a few people who do not apparently respond to vital points. When working with pressure points, I like to think in terms of normal distribution, as in a bell curve. If we were to use the percentages of a normal bell curve we could expect 84.13 percent of the individuals you work with to react very strongly to any pressure point you choose to work with. An additional 13.6 percent will exhibit a reaction to some but not all vital points, for a total of 97.73 percent of the population who will experience some reaction. Some points will be more susceptible to attack than others; it will be a matter of experience and guidance to determine which points to attack. There are a small number (.11 percent) of individuals who apparently do not respond to vital points. The chance that you will encounter such a person is very small. If you find you are having trouble getting the expected response from your partner, there may be several factors involved. The first, and most likely, is a lack of experience in locating vital points and using vital-point techniques. Other reasons you may have difficulty getting results could be that the individual has been in an accident or had surgery that has resulted in the link being destroyed. It is more likely that a person would not react strongly to a particular vital point, but they would react to other vital points.

As a basic rule, you will find that the larger the person or the larger the bone, the larger the vital point will be. It is much easier to perform vital-point techniques on large male opponent than on a small child or a small woman. Children will not have developed all of their vital points to the point where they can be used for these types of techniques. Women will have these vital points developed, but they will usually be much smaller than a man's. It will require much greater accuracy and precision when executing techniques on them. If you are able to find the points accurately, the strike will require less pressure than you would use on your male counterparts.

Women, small men, and children in fact are at somewhat of an advantage with vital point techniques. Because they are smaller than their opponents, they will be able to make sharper turns and use their bodies at sharper angles. With a sharper turn or angle of attack, you can greatly increase the pain of your opponent.

An additional way to increase the pain of a joint lock is to increase the tension on the joint and then to create torque on the area. One simple way to do this is to lower your stance when you apply pressure. This is one of the reasons why stances change height in a kata. The more upright the stance, the more mobility you will have. These stances are used in the beginning segments of a self-defense situation. When you wish to increase the damage to your opponent, you will lower your stance and shift your body weight. In practice, if you attempt a technique utilizing this concept, you must do it very slowly and be aware of your opponent's reaction.

 # ANALYSIS

Those skilled at making the enemy move do so by creating a situation to which he must conform.

— Sun Tzu

Conceptual Elements Required for Critical Analysis of Kata

The intent of this book is help you look at kata from a different viewpoint and to develop effective self-defense techniques for yourself. Once you look at kata from what may be an unorthodox view, you may begin to develop your own set of techniques suited to your particular needs. Because this book addresses the self-defense aspect of kata, consideration of sporting or recreational uses will not be addressed. This is not to say that such applications are not valid or important, only that such a discussion is beyond the scope of this book.

To critically analyze kata, we will need a group of tools or concepts (some of which have been discussed) to explore the intricacies of the self-defense techniques found in traditional kata. With this approach, it is likely that we will find solutions, or techniques, outside our core system. We can organize our thoughts and insights so as to integrate various techniques into effective self-defense methods. When looking at kata with an eye to identifying various techniques, the initial step is to isolate the particular movement in question. At this point, we need to develop various scenarios in an attempt to develop an effective technique.

Initially, we must determine from which direction the attack will be directed. At its simplest level, we can expect an attack to come from one of three directions: front, side, or back. Once we have determined to look at a technique from one of these basic directions, we then need to make a further decision as to the type of attack being initiated. While the number of attacks may seem enormous, I think we can began to categorize attacks with some very simple concepts. I will preface our analysis of attacks by stipulating that these techniques are simplified for the purposes of examination. Further, for the purposes of this book, all bunkai are considered to be against a single unarmed opponent. This is not to discount the possibility that bunkai could take place with multiple armed opponents.

Further, the basic assumption for this book will be that you are being attacked by either a hand or foot technique, and there is only a single assailant. For this discussion, hand techniques will include all types of punches, back fist strikes, elbow strikes, grabs, or any offensive technique that makes use of any part of your hand or arm. I would like to apply this same broad type of definition to include any kick, sweep, thrust, or use of your leg in an offensive manner, when referring to foot techniques.

We can further subdivide hand attacks according to the following types of attacks with the hand. These divisions may not contain all of the possible permutations, but the vast majority of offensive actions can be covered by these divisions of attacks:

I.   Grab (from the front, side, or rear)

1. same side grab

2. cross-hand grab

3. double-hand grab

From this major group of grabbing techniques we can then project areas of the body that would most likely be attacked with a grab. They are:

1. Wrist

2. Lower arm (from the wrist to elbow)

3. Upper arm (from elbow to shoulder)

4. Chest

5. Head

6. Neck

It is possible that you would be grabbed by the leg or from your waist down but the probability of this occurring would seem to be remote. Therefore, the majority of your time could be devoted to defense against these attacks, and a minimal amount of time could be spent on other types of attacks. When an attacker grabs your wrist, more often than not, his intent is to immobilize you in some way. An untrained individual will often "freeze" in place once they have been grabbed. Of course a grab in many situations is a precursor to other types of attacks.

II.   Push (from the front, side, or rear)

1. Same side push

2. Cross-side push

3. Double-hand push

Pushes would more than likely occur with either a single- or double-hand push. It is unlikely you would encounter a cross-side push, since this puts the attacker in a very poor position. By crossing the direction of his push he will move his other arm farther away from your body, which will make it virtually impossible for him to grab, push, or punch you with that hand. When you are pushed, your opponent's intent, many times, is to off-balance you and to intimidate you. Pushes tend to be directed at your upper body, where your opponent can generate his maximum power. If he were to push at your stomach or the lower portion of your body he would not be able to effectively generate power.

III.   Punching, striking, or kicking techniques (from the front, side, or rear)

1.   Same side punch/strike/kick

2.   Cross-side punch/strike/kick

3.   Double-punch/strike/kick

Strikes and kicks are used to cause damage to one's opponent. Hand techniques will often be delivered to the head and upper portion of your body. I believe it is instinctive to punch at a level that is somewhat in line with one's shoulder. It seems to be intuitive that punches at this level will allow an individual to generate the maximum amount of power from the punch. Many times you will find attacks delivered to your head and especially to the nose and mouth. I speculate that, at an unconscious level, punches to the mouth are a way of stopping verbal action or reaction. Take for example a situation in which two people are preparing to fight in a bar or pub. Many times, prior to the first punch being thrown, you will hear the individuals yelling back and forth. A punch would likely be delivered to the mouth in an attempt to keep the other individual from further verbal assault. When we look at kicks from untrained individuals, these will most likely be delivered against your groin and legs. Without training, it is unlikely an individual will have the flexibility or technique to deliver an effective kick to the upper portion of a person's body. While a skilled martial artist could deliver kicks to various locations of the body, the probability that you will be attacked by a fellow martial artist seems to be low.

I know these are very broad categories of attacks, but as an exercise, try to write down some type of grabs that do not involve one of the above scenarios. I would wager that you will find that the majority of situations you can conceive of fall under these broad categories. Therefore, it would seem wise to develop a set of core techniques based on these probable attacks. As you develop skill in the martial arts, additional techniques can be incorporated into your repertoire. Providing that your primary reason for practicing a martial art is self-defense you can tailor your practice in accordance with Pareto's 80-20 law. You would spend 80 percent of your time practicing against those attacks that you are most likely to face and the remaining 20 percent of your training time in other areas.

When looking at attacks, such as grabs, pushes, and strikes, there are several important points to remember. What is the difference between a grab to the chest, a push to the chest, and a punch to the chest? I would like to point out some of the differences and some of the similarities. As outlined above, the intent behind a grab, push, and strike is different, and, as a consequence, the hand formation will be different. When using the grab and push, your opponent will in most cases have his hand open when his arm comes in your direction. When dealing with the untrained fighter, you are most likely going to face a closed hand. So the hand formation will probably be different with each of these three major groups of attacks. The speed of your opponent's hand will probably vary to some small degree; the grab will probably be the slowest, with the punch being the fastest. In addition, the time your opponent's hand will stay within your zone of defense will differ. A punch will be thrown and immediately withdrawn, so as to be able to deliver another punch. Pushes will tend to stay near your body for a split second before they are retracted for another push or possibly a punch. Grabs, by their nature, will remain static on some part of your body, although your opponent may use this as an opportunity to pull or push you off-balance. It is important to note that any of these attacks can have the same point of contact, and, if so, the direction taken by the arm will be the same.

Why is it important to consider these differences and similarities? When learning new techniques, it will be less difficult to develop skill against a grab than against a punch. Likewise, a push will require less skill to defend against than a punch. So, from a teaching and learning perspective, it seems to me that we should develop a curriculum that first develops skill against grabs, second against pushes, and third against strikes/kicking techniques. Of course we need not exclusively practice only one category of technique. But if we concentrate on developing skills in a logical and progressive manner, I feel our limited time will be well spent.

To start with, practice the technique slowly and with care. Begin with techniques that center around *tori* (attacker) grabbing *uki* (receiver) from a relatively static position. Once you gain familiarity with a technique, you will be able to perform it as a defense against a more dynamic attack. Your opponent can attack with greater speed and force. You will be able to respond faster and with more controlled reactions. Of course it is very important that you exercise all due care when practicing with a partner. These techniques are designed to dislocate or break the joint of your opponent. While it is possible to control an individual with these techniques, the intent and purpose is to break the joint or dislocate it.

Once you reach the point where you can defend yourself from a grab with these techniques, begin to execute the same techniques just as your opponent begins to make contact with your body. Try to apply the technique before he can secure a grip, and, as before, increase the speed and intensity of your defense to match that of your opponent's attack. Soon you will find yourself able to make use of these techniques in defending from both a push or grab. Then it comes time to increase the intensity of your opponent's attack to that of a strike. You will have laid the groundwork for this type of practice with your previous practice. If your preparation has been adequate, you will find your progress to be rapid.

It is important to remember that you must develop skill in the martial arts to make use of vital points. These points require an effective delivery system; they are not magic and cannot be used alone. The analogy I like to use is: your martial arts skills are like a rocket, and vital points are the nuclear warheads. If you do not have a reliable and accurate delivery system, the warheads will not be delivered to your opponent.

It is vital that you gain expertise and skill in a traditional form of martial arts. It does not matter if the system is karate, tae kwon do, aikido, tai chi chuan, jujitsu, or any other art. From my research, I feel confident that all systems of martial arts have made use of vital points. When I look at the early texts on judo and jujitsu, many of the books have charts and diagrams of vital points. Others may only speak of places to strike that will cause damage to the individual, but vital points are utilized in these texts. These books are in English and date back to 1903.

In my earlier work, *Martial Arts for the University: A Textbook for Basic Judo, Ju-jitsu, Karate, Tae Kwon Do, Modern Arnis, and Vital Points* (Clark 1992, pp. 1–5), I made the argument that vital-point techniques were withheld intentionally from the Western martial artist. It is quite clear that Koyama and Minami (1913) state that "the knowledge of jiu jitsu [*sic*] has only recently been made general in Japan. . . upper classes, jealous lest their influence over the populace should wane, tried to keep it to themselves" (p. 6). I argue that the more esoteric techniques in the martial arts were reserved for the Oriental practitioner. Koyama and Minami (1913) give credence to this assertion when they state "there are some jui jitus [*sic*] maneuvers that have never been explained to Europeans or Americans—and probably they never will be. These death blows are remarkable. Some are delivered to the spine, others on the neck and head, and two on the face. There are almost numberless maneuvers that temporarily paralyze nerves and nerve centers, and others that stop circulation of the blood in various parts of the body" (pp. 5–6). Other authors echo the statements of Koyama and Minami. One such individual is Vairamuttu (1954, p. 21); he suggested "the real secrets of advanced jujitsu, which are so greatly treasured by the Japanese and imparted under a veil of secrecy to pupils of unquestionable moral character, have ever been divulged to occidentals, is very much open to doubt." The secrets that Vairamuttu alludes to were techniques that made use of vital points. He also believed that the revival techniques used to restore an individual to consciousness were an even more closely held secret.

This veil of secrecy extended to the art of aikido promulgated by Morihei Ueshiba. Stevens (1987) translated a privately circulated textbook by Ueshiba, *Budo* (1938), in which he states "this manual is not to be shown to non-Japanese" (p. 78). Any number of texts of this time refer to the secrecy associated with the teaching of vital points. What I had failed to notice was that all of these texts were referring to vital-point techniques and by doing so were in fact being open in the dissemination of the very information I felt they were withholding. They did show charts of vital points and discussed in detail various techniques that would make use of vital points. While there were not a large number of points discussed nor were there a great number of techniques described, they were to be found. After World War II, when judo and jujitsu became more popular in the United States and other countries, the use of vital points seems to have diminished. Virtually every book printed before World War II detailed vital-point techniques. Admittedly, they did not go into great detail or depth, but the material was there.

I am strongly convinced that, as sports techniques were introduced, the martial applications of vital points were removed. I do not believe that the intent was to keep these techniques secret from the occidental practitioner of the martial arts. I believe that these techniques were removed for the safety of the students. If students were practicing predominantly sporting techniques, they would have little or no use for the more dangerous techniques of self-defense. Since instructors did not teach vital points for the sporting applications, it seems likely they were dropped from the curriculum. Those students who were trained in the sporting applications then became instructors themselves and were not well versed in this particular aspect of the martial arts.

Once the martial arts were no longer practiced purely for self-defense, the vital-point applications would have diminished. Even some of those whom we consider to be the "old masters" may have been exposed to primarily the sporting applications of the martial arts.

E. J. Harrison, in his book *The Manual of Karate* (1959) stated "seeing that in karate, unlike judo, very few methods can be safely demonstrated to their logical conclusion without risk of seriously injuring an opponent and must therefore be halted a split second before reaching their target; special importance is naturally ascribed to study and practice of the relevant karate kata, or forms. It should be added that, obviously, when kata is being demonstrated by only one karateka, the risk of injury is no longer involved. It must be admitted that when compared with the judo kata the karate kata tends to appear monotonous and lacking the latter's spectacular appeal and dynamism. Nonetheless within their own and as an ideal empirical means to an end, i.e., to be used for the possible obliteration of a potential enemy, the karate kata cannot fail to impress an intelligent objective observer. And the deeper one delves into the technical details of these forms, the less conscious one becomes of the initial impression of their monotony" (p. 60).

In somewhat the same light, Hironori Otsuka (1997) states "I personally favor Naihanchi. It is not interesting to the eye, but it is extremely difficult to use. Naihanchi increases in difficulty with more time spent practicing it, however, there is something 'deep' about it. It is fundamental to any movement that requires reaction, I believe. Some people may call me foolish for my belief. I, however, preferred this over all else and I incorporated it into my movement. This has three katas, Shodan, Ni-dan, San-dan but the last two are almost useless" (p. 72). I find the statement of Otsuka quite puzzling. He speaks of kata being alive; he states "Kata is a fundamental aspect of martial arts and hence is unyieldingly important. It can never just be 'form.' It is essential to train for the 'living' form" (p. 21). I believe Otsuka understood karate was inseparable from kata, yet I am not convinced he had an understanding of bunkai that allowed him to see the value of naihanchi, nidan, and sandan. Clearly, there is an abundance of self-defense techniques to be found in all of the various kata. However, for some reason, he seemed to feel that naihanchi, nidan, and sandan were virtually useless to the practitioner of karate.

Nakayama voiced a similar sentiment about the naihanchi (teki) kata. He stated: "Since these kata are rather monotonous, turn the head briskly and strongly" (p. 106). I find it quite amazing that such pioneering martial artists as Otsuka and Nakayama would feel these kata were so dreadfully boring that they were dismissive of them.

Harrison (1959) states: "It is essential that every student of karate should familiarize himself with the vital spots (Kyusho in Japanese) of the human body. Lacking this knowledge, and if engaged in a life and death struggle with a powerful opponent, his inability to strike the proper target, i.e., the vital spots, that is points on the body, might lead to his discomfiture and even to a sticky end! In both karate and judo vital spots may be briefly described as that part of human body which the karateka assails with hands, fists, wrists, elbows, knees, heels and toes in various ways for the purpose either of knocking out his victim or if necessary killing him out right. To this laudable end the utmost precision in locating the vital spots and knowledge of varying degrees of sensitivity involved in every case are clearly indispensable" (p. 128).

Funakoshi (1988) states in *Karate Do Nyumon* "if your practice consists of no more than moving in your arms and legs, you might as well be studying dance. You'll never come to know the true meaning of karate" (p. 43). Nagamine (1976) in *The Essence of Okinawan Karate Do* states "karate is beginning to lose its value in martial arts" (p. 26). These authors were reacting to the sporting nature of karate that was being promulgated in the early 1920s in Japan. Texts written in this time period indicate the use of simple block/punch techniques. In other words, as an opponent punched, you would block with one hand and counterattack with the opposite. In these examples, the punch that was being countered would be 12 to 18 inches away from the defender. It is quite probable that no block would have been needed in such an attack. Even with full extension, the punch would never have reached the face of the opponent. Such a technique would not be practical in a real self-defense situation. Admittedly, these books were attempting to teach individuals to block oncoming blows. At its most basic level, it is not necessary to teach an individual how to block. This is a reflexive action instinctive to all human beings. To prove this point, you need only direct a punch or kick to the groin of an untrained individual; you'll find an immediate response to your attack.

Kata was designed by warriors to practice techniques they would use in combat. Their lives depended upon the effectiveness of their techniques and their ability to quickly apply them. It would have been the intent of these individuals to use techniques that would rapidly incapacitate their opponents or even kill them. To incapacitate their opponents, they would have needed to dislocate, break, or control the opponents' joints in such a way as to produce pain compliance. Where possible, these individuals would have looked for techniques that would knock out or kill their opponents in the most expeditious manner. They would not have been interested in techniques that would have caused delayed reactions, such as the fabled "delayed death touch"; only techniques that offered immediate, predictable, and effective results would have been practiced. Kata gave these individuals the ability to repeat techniques hundreds of times. Constant repetition of techniques will build a conditioned response for the individual. In psychology, it is a well-established maxim that people revert to previously learned behavior in moments of stress. Martial arts practice is designed to extinguish ineffective patterns and replace them with new and effective responses.

If we look briefly at common techniques found in virtually every martial arts system, we can identify a basic fallacy in low-level applications from kata. Most systems utilize a "down block." This block typically has one hand slightly below your waist and the arm extended at approximately a 45-degree angle. The opposite hand is resting with the fist at the side of the body, normally pressing against the belt. The basic explanation given for this technique is someone is punching or kicking at your lower stomach or groin, and you are deflecting the attack with your extended arm and preparing to counterattack with the hand that is resting at your waist. If you were to critically analyze this technique, you would notice that your hand position leaves you open to counterattack by your opponent. While it is possible to block an attack to your lower section with this technique, the placement of your rear hand would not appear to the effective. It does not require an extensive knowledge of the martial arts to deduce that this explanation leaves something to be desired. No one in full possession of his or her faculties would engage in a deadly confrontation with one hand positioned by the waist ready to attack. It would be prudent to have both hands in a position that would allow you to attack as well as defend yourself.

When we analyze kata for self-defense techniques, it is imperative that we recognize that both hands are being utilized in the techniques. It is highly unlikely that you would have your hands in such a position as to render one hand useless. Just as we would attempt to make use of both of our hands in a sparring situation, we should remember that in self-defense we would attempt to maximize our defensive capability by utilizing all parts of our body efficiently. Understanding kata does not present a major problem; it just takes a "key." In everyday language, a key serves the function of unlocking a door. A door bars your entrance into a house or room; you need a key to unlock the door so that you may enter. The key for understanding kata is really quite simple. Once your thought process breaks away from block/punch combinations, you have the ability to view techniques in a different light. Some key points for understanding kata are:

1. Each movement in a kata is designed to cause serious bodily harm to your opponent in the shortest amount of time possible. Anytime your hand reaches out to "block" an aggressive motion of your opponent, you should be striking or grabbing vital points. This will have the effect of stopping or redirecting your opponent's attack. If you have accurately struck or grabbed a vital point you will elicit pain, temporary paralysis, dislocation of the joint, or a knockout.

2. Two hands are utilized in self-defense techniques. If someone throws a basketball aimed at the center of your chest, do you attempt to catch the ball with one hand or two? My guess is that you would use both hands. It is a natural reflex of the body to use both hands when catching the basketball. Likewise, when someone is punching or kicking at you, your natural tendency will be to use both hands for a defensive maneuver. Many techniques suggest that both hands are being used simultaneously, one to strike a vital point of the attacking limb and the other to strike points on the body. Or, one hand could be used to deflect the oncoming attack and the other hand for securing a grip for a lock or a throw.

3. Vital points are always being utilized in your defense. It does not matter what you're doing, you should always be grabbing or striking vital points of your opponent. Consider that when you grip your opponent's arm or wrist in a self-defense situation. Your hand invariably will fall near points that could be utilized to elicit a pain response from your opponent. Not to make use of these points seems foolhardy. The only way you'll be able to apply these points

in a self-defense situation will be to continuously practice these points in the dojo.

4. Kata will give you the angle and direction of attack. When you analyze the movements in a kata, you will find many applications that could be useful. When you attempt these techniques in the dojo, the only actually effective techniques will be those that still resemble the movement in the kata. If your self-defense technique changes so drastically that you cannot recognize the kata movement, I would suggest that this would not be a viable bunkai for that particular movement.

Every movement in a traditional kata has the potential of being an effective self-defense technique. To discover their secrets requires an understanding of vital points and their function in conjunction with a broad base of information from various martial arts systems.

KATA APPLICATIONS

Those skilled in war bring the enemy to the field of battle and are not brought there by him.

—Sun Tzu

In martial arts circles, there has long been a position that touts the concept that there is no advantage to being the first to attack. This concept puzzled me for a long time. If you are in close quarters with an opponent who possesses good hand speed and is skilled, he would be able to land a punch before you could react. If the aggressor in this situation is adept in the use of vital points, he would probably defeat you before you could mount any resistance. "There is no first attack in karate," makes it seems that you must be grabbed, shoved, punched, or kicked before you can respond with any defensive measure.

Karl von Clausewitz, in his classic text *On War*, helped clarify this concept for me. In one of his opening paragraphs on attack in defense he asks "What is the concept of defense? The parrying of the blow" (p. 357). He goes on to state "A battle is defensive if we await the attack—await, that is, the appearance of the enemy in front of our lines and within range. A campaign is defensive if we wait for our theater of operations to be invaded" (p. 357). This concept struck a chord with me. During my time working as a security policeman in the United States Air Force, we were taught there was a defensive parameter around your body. If that space was invaded, you were placing yourself in danger. So, during interrogations, we always attempted to maintain distance from our suspects. We wanted to be far enough away from them that they would not be able to initiate an attack without our being able to respond. Yet, we wanted to be close enough so that we could apply physical restraint if necessary.

This concept seems to fit well with Clausewitz's concept that we await the appearance of the enemy within range. In other words if we were not being aggressive or attacking, once the aggressor came within striking distance they were fair game. Because we did not initiate the attack, any response we would make to the aggressive movements of our opponents would come under the heading of "defense." Even though our defensive tactics might appear to be offensive, they would in fact be defensive in nature. Thus, a defensive strategy can be used if we are not initiating the attack, rather than waiting within our own space for the individual to invade that area. Any offensive action we may take while awaiting the assault can be seen as defensive. "So the defensive form of war is not a simple shield, but a shield made up of well-directed blows" (ibid. 357).

Clausewitz mentions numerous times in his book that "defense is simply the stronger form of war, the one that makes the enemies' defeat more certain" (ibid. 380). This simple concept requires that our defense be sufficiently strong so as to be able to place our opponent in an untenable position. Therefore, when we analyze kata with the intention of developing effective bunkai, we must work from the position that we are being attacked. This attack can be envisioned in numerous scenarios. In this chapter, there will be examples of how the same movement from a kata can be used against a punch, a push, or a grab. There will also be illustrations of how the same movement can be used against attacks from the front or from the rear. In the same light, you can develop techniques that utilize these movements against attacks from the side or even against multiple opponents.

I've chosen movements from kata that are utilized in Japanese and Okinawan karate. The same kata were used in the early versions of tae kwon do; and the same forms are currently being used by tang soo do, moo do kwan, and some systems of tae kwon do still utilize these forms. When applicable, I will list the common name of the kata in Japanese or

Okinawan karate, and the Korean name. For some of the examples, I have used multiple techniques from the same kata to illustrate how movements can be developed from one technique to the next. I'm sure there will be stylistic differences among the various systems; however, the gross movements should be somewhat similar. If, in your system, you do not have these kata, perhaps you'll have movements that appear to be similar to the ones presented in this chapter.

KUSANKU - KANKU - KUNG SAN GUN — SHUTO UKE 1

Kusanku is considered to be one of the primary kata in the martial arts community. Within this kata you will find movements found in the five Pinan (Heian/Pyung-Ahn) kata as well as in other kata. Some speculate that Anko Itosu used this kata to create the five Pinan kata taught in the school system of Okinawa. It seems that he may have decided to take a larger kata and break it into smaller, more manageable units for the students.

The opening movement of Kusanku offers several interesting bunkai for us to study. The hand motions start with your hands low and in front of your belt. If you extend your arms, and slightly bend them, your fingertips will come close together (Figure 1). The next movement is sometimes represented as "viewing the moon," where your hands are raised to head level and your fingertips are almost touching (Figure 2). The next motion is "the double-knife hand block" or Shuto Uki (Figure 3). The first motion in the sequence can be used as a self-defense technique against a "full nelson." If you have your thumbs pointed in a forward direction (Figure 4) your opponent will easily be able to apply this technique. A simple defense against a full nelson is to bend your arms slightly, rotate your thumbs back toward your body, and press down with your palms (Figure 5). When you perform this motion, your opponent will find it extremely difficult to raise your arms. He will find a great deal of difficulty in getting his arms past your shoulder area. This offers an opportunity to attack your opponent's hand with a joint lock. The joint lock could be described as similar to an upside down Sankyo. The wrist is turned so that the little finger rotates in toward the body. With

Sankyo, the elbow faces toward the ceiling and the fingers point toward the ground. In this variant, the fingers are pointing either to the left or right, and the elbow points in the opposite direction; the forearm is horizontal. This lock is applied by placing your thumb between your opponent's thumb and forefinger. The tip of your thumb should rest on the knuckle of his forefinger, and the tip of your middle finger should be at the end of his little finger. Pressure is applied by pressing the little finger back and toward the thumb, and at the same time rotating the opponent's hand toward his body. If you grab your opponent's left hand with your right hand, you will twist the wrist in a counterclockwise motion. Your opponent's wrist would have been turned in a clockwise motion if you had grabbed his right hand with your left hand. Another way in which to increase the level of pain is to keep the opponent's wrist as straight as possible.

Once your opponent begins to react to the pain (Figure 6), extend your left foot slightly and turn your body. This forces your opponent to offer the side of the neck as a target. There are a number of locations on the head and neck that offer you potential targets. One such point is the "triple warmer"

(Figure 9). This point is located in the cavity below the ear at the temporal mandibular joint. If you strike this point and your opponent's mouth is open, it is highly likely you will dislocate the jaw, and knock him out. If you were able to apply a great deal of pain to your opponent's wrist and fingers, you

may find him shouting out in pain. This would of course cause him to have his mouth open and susceptible to dislocation. Funakoshi (1983, p. 243) states that the result of such a strike would be a loss of consciousness due to trauma of the cranial nerves and spinal cord. There would also be a loss of sensory and motor function of the body.

The finger lock used in this example relies on applying pressure to the little finger. Pressure is applied with your middle finger on the tip of your opponent's little finger, first you press back and then press the little finger toward the thumb of your opponent's hand. This creates a tremendous amount of pressure on your opponent and will cause a great deal of pain. You must be careful not to wrap your whole hand around your opponent's, to do so will reduce the amount of pressure you can apply to this lock. This same principle can be applied to other locks that make use of similar hand positions. For example, with Sanykyo, you will be able to use the little finger in this same manner.

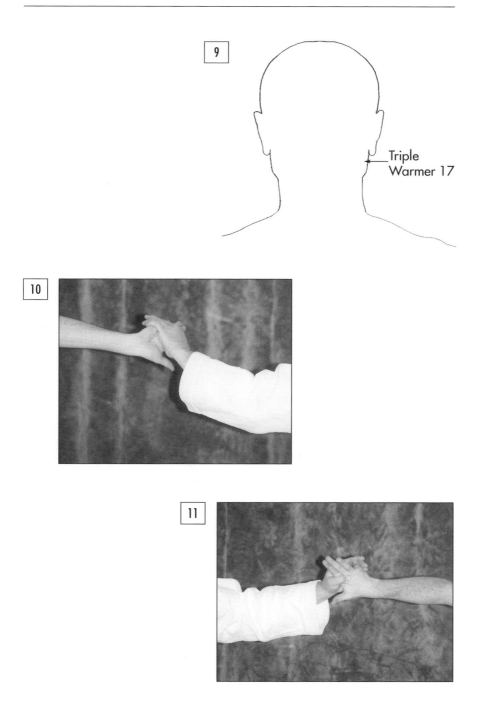

Triple
Warmer 17

KUSANKU - KANKU - KUNG SAN GUNG — SHUTO UKE 2

A common technique in most systems is the double-knife hand strike (Figures 12 and 13). While there are many variations for this technique, an interesting application for the double-knife hand involves a strike to vital points on the head and neck area along with a leg lock technique.

As your opponent begins to punch with his right hand (Figure. 14) step forward with your right foot so that your opponent's foot is next to yours (Figure 15). At the same time raise your right hand to deflect Uke's punch and prepare to strike vital points in the head and neck area (Figure 16). Use the motion of your right hand to push your opponent's body in a counterclockwise manner, and press his right arm down with your left hand. If you pay careful attention to your foot position, it is possible to lock your opponent's leg in such a manner as to unbalance him. To do this, you must have your foot very close to his foot and place the outside of your right leg against his leg. Then, if you press in on his leg, you can break his balance and cause his body to turn even more. This will expose the vital points of the head and neck area and reduce your opponent's ability to defend against such a strike (Figure 17).

14

15

16

17

PINAN - HEIAN - PYUNG AHN 4

In Pinan 4, there is short sequence of movements in which you have your forward knife hand at eye level and your rear knife hand at your head with your palm facing outward (Figure 18). Many times the bunkai given for this motion is that you're defending your face from attacks delivered by two separate individuals. While it is possible to defend your face from attacks using either hand, it is unlikely that you would be attacked simultaneously by two individuals.

The next movement in the kata is a low X-block with your fists closed (Figure 19). The bunkai for these techniques typically is a defense against a kick to the lower section of your body. Again, this technique could be performed as described. But such bunkai does not take into consideration your opponent's ability to use his hands to attack your upper body. I do not wish to demean any bunkai an instructor or organization currently uses. I merely wish to offer alternate explanations for these movements. If we critically analyze this type of explanation, it is clear that there are practical problems with it. Quite obviously such a technique could work, and I am sure people have utilized this technique exactly as described. Does that mean that the easy explanation is the only or best explanation? Of course not, there can be multiple effective techniques derived from these two movements from Pinan 4.

Understanding that there can be multiple explanations for each movement or sequence of movements in kata, it would seem prudent to seek as many explanations as possible. From these multiple explanations, you would be able to select techniques that best fit your needs and expectations for self-defense.

With the following sequences, I would like to offer some alternate explanations for these few movements. I do not claim that these are the original bunkai envisioned by the individual who first developed these two movements in kata. Nor, will I claim any of the bunkai demonstrated in this book gives the original intent of any master. With these explanations I've attempted to utilize "out of the box thinking" to give a variety of explanations. Perhaps one of the techniques I describe is an original application; it really doesn't matter, since these techniques do come from various martial arts systems.

PINAN - HEIAN - PYUNG AHN 4 — JUJI NAGE

The following techniques are performed with the person attacking from the rear, and later the same movement will be used to defend yourself when your opponent is facing you. By using techniques that can be applied from the front and the rear we're stepping outside of the box and looking at these two movements from a variety of angles. Sometimes when we have a movement in kata that seems a bit "strange," it may be useful to apply the principles demonstrated in the following sequence of techniques. In other words, when we attempt to analyze the movements of the kata, we envision that our attacker may be coming from the rear or the side. While you may have a technique that's valid from one direction, you may discover that the technique would be even more effective if it were to come from another angle.

In the following situations, your opponent has grabbed you from the rear, his right arm is around your neck grabbing your collar, and his left hand is grabbing your right wrist (Figure 20). At the moment you feel

yourself being grabbed, widen your stance slightly and bend your knees. You'll wish to turn your head toward the elbow of your opponent to mitigate the effect of his arm choking you. At the same time circle the hand that is grabbed toward your center, turning your palm down with your thumb facing toward your body (Figure 21). You should also slightly bend your arm at the same time. This will have the effect of loosening your opponent's grip on your wrist; you should be able to maintain some contact with your hand at this time. Once your grip has been loosened, raise your left hand toward your head and continue turning your body into your opponent in a clockwise motion (Figure 22). Move your right hand up toward his left hand, which is still gripping your left wrist. With your right hand, grip your opponent's left with a wrist lock, Sankyo (Figure 23). At this point you could continue the wrist lock into a number of different techniques. If you continue with your technique, you can grab your opponent's right wrist with your left hand. Push his right arm above his left elbow (Figure 25) and apply pressure at the joint. This forces your opponent to lose his balance toward his right-front section (Figure 26). If you continue your motion, stepping out with your left foot, you can throw your opponent with juji-nage (Figure 27).

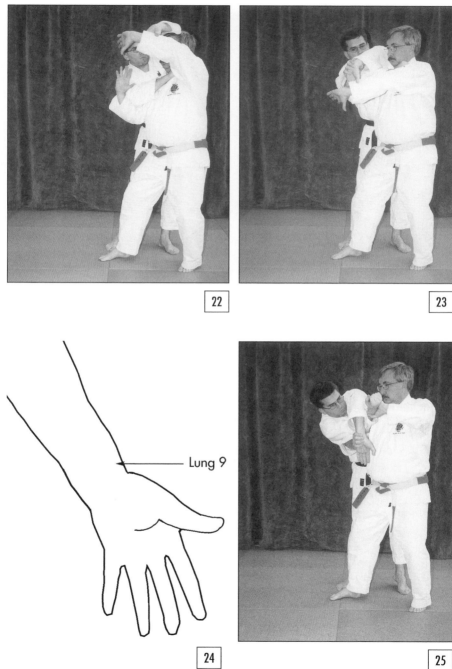

22

23

Lung 9

24

25

26

27

Pinan - Heian - Pyung Ahn 4 — Kubi Nage

From a similar attack as that previously described (Figure 28), raise your left hand to head height. You're right hand should come up so that your fingertips will almost meet (Figure 29); for illustration purposes only, my hand is in front of my opponent's arm. This was done only to show that your hands would be in the same relative position as the movement in the kata. You would, however, place your palm underneath the chin of your opponent and grab the top of his head with your left hand. You would then step forward and twist the neck in such a way as to throw him forward (Figure 30) using the low X-block as the throwing technique. This technique does present a degree of danger to your partner in practice. If you wish to practice this technique, you must fully discuss the throw and the confidence of your partner's skill in breakfall techniques. You must execute this technique slowly and with due caution. The danger that is present with the application of this technique is obvious.

28

29

30

PINAN - HEIAN - PYUNG AHN 4 — SAME-SIDE WRIST GRAB 1

In this sequence your opponent has grabbed your wrists from the rear (Figure 31). At the moment your opponent makes contact with your body, drop your hips and widen your stance. Rotate your palms so your thumbs face toward your body, and push your elbows out slightly so that your arm has a slight bend (Figure 32).

Remember, when you do these techniques, to mimic the movements in the kata because the kata will give you the correct body motions.

Shift your body weight to your rear leg and duck your head under your opponent's left arm (Figure 33). This moves your body slightly to the side and disturbs the balance of your opponent. If you pull your hands slightly forward and up, you will be able to keep your opponent slightly off-balance.

31

32

33   34

Turn your body in toward your opponent and grab his right hand with your left. Circle your right fingers and thumb over the top of the forearm of your opponent and use a "nikyo" to begin a control technique. You could, of course, break your opponent's wrist as you apply this joint lock (Figure 34). A close-up of your hand position can be seen in Figure 37. As you begin to apply pressure with this lock, your opponent will probably react by dropping to his knees and bending away from the pain.

Continue to apply pressure on the wrist by circling your hand back and toward your body. Figures 38 and 39 give a close-up view of how your hand should circle your opponent's wrist. In this example I've extended my forefinger in an attempt to show the direction in which pressure should be applied. Please note that my forefinger is pointing back at my body; this places an extreme amount of pressure on your opponent's wrist.

Continue the pressure on your opponent's wrist and step forward with your left leg. When you perform this technique you'll notice that your hands are crossed and low in front of your body. Your hand position will be similar to that of a low X-block (Figure 35 and 36).

35 36

PINAN - HEIAN - PYUNG AHN 4 — SAME-SIDE WRIST GRAB 2

In this sequence of techniques, your opponent has grabbed your left wrist with his right hand (Figure 37). At the moment he makes contact with your wrist pivot on your left leg and step forward with your right leg, roll your left hand over the top of your opponent's hand and lock your arm to your body. Do not try to pull your opponent with your arm, but allow the movement of your upper body and legs to turn you, keeping your left arm in the same relative position. This will have the effect of pulling your opponent off-balance without having to use the strength of your arm. Strike Heart 2 with your right palm heel (Figure 39). This will cause your opponent's balance to break to the rear, or may even knock him to the ground. If you make contact at this point, you can have very strong effects from this strike alone. It is even possible that some individuals will be knocked unconscious from the strike.

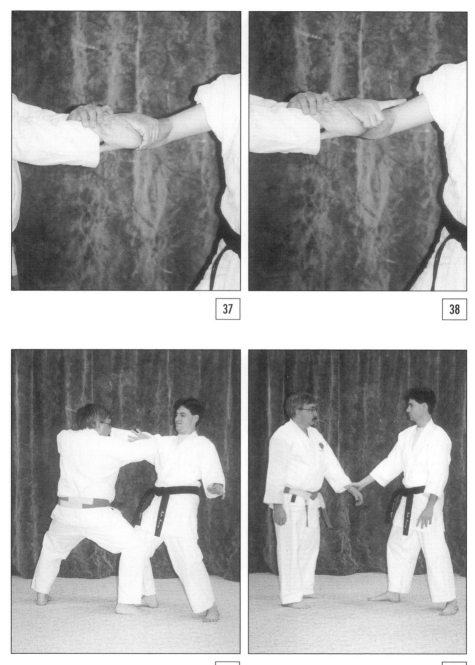

37

38

39

39a

39b   39c

PINAN - HEIAN - PYUNG AHN 4 — SAME-SIDE WRIST GRAB 3

In this sequence of movements your opponent has grabbed you in exactly the same manner as in the preceding technique. The major difference in this technique is that it targets Stomach 9 (Figure 43). Additionally, your right hand (Figure 41) would strike this point in a more direct fashion. You would not make the larger circular palm heel strike, but rather strike with the knife hand.

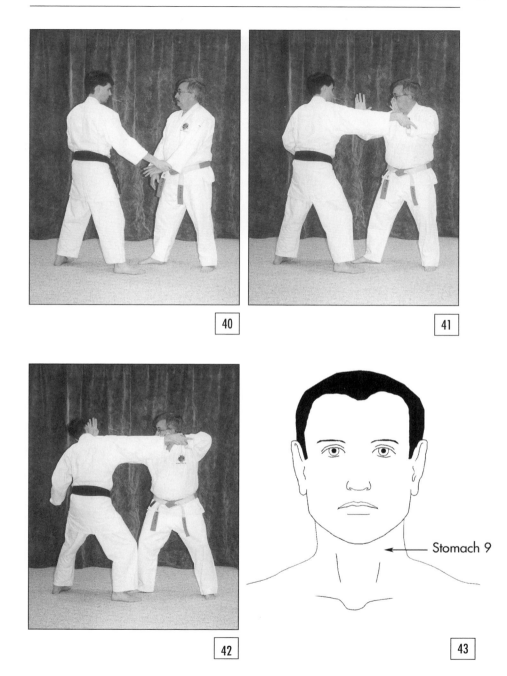

40

41

42

43

Stomach 9

PINAN - HEIAN - PYUNG AHN 4 — SAME-SIDE WRIST GRAB TO ARM BAR 3

This sequence of photographs is designed to illustrate "fault-tolerant technique." As previously illustrated with the same basic movement from Pinan 4, there are a number of targets and techniques available to you. If you attempted a strike at any of the previous targets (Stomach 9, Small Intestine 17, or Heart 2), you will have noticed that the opponent did not punch or attempt to counter the technique with his left hand. Once again your opponent attacks by grabbing your left wrist with his right hand (Figure 44). Once you begin to withdraw your right hand, your opponent initiates a punch toward your face. From repetitive movement when practicing this kata, you instinctively bring your right hand up and away from of your body, covering your face; redirect your opponent's punch with your right hand in a counterclockwise direction (Figure 45). Withdraw your left hand from your opponent's grip and grab his left wrist with your left hand (Figure 46). Simply roll your right arm behind your opponent's elbow and press down on the elbow (Figure 47). Notice that the pressure is being exerted on the arm in such away that the attacker is being forced over his little toe. One of the

44

45

easiest ways to cause an opponent to lose his balance is to push his weight in the direction of the little toe. This is especially effective if he has planted his weight on that leg. An example can be seen in Figure 46; You'll notice that the right foot is planted firmly on the ground. However, the right foot has contact only at the ball of the foot. So by pushing his weight over his little toe, it will require much less effort to take him to the ground (Figure 48).

46

47

48

PINAN - HEIAN - PYUNG AHN 4 — DEFENSE AGAINST A PUNCH TO THE HEAD 1

The usefulness of a fault-tolerance technique is further demonstrated in this sequence. Both you and your opponent are standing close together with both of your chests facing in the same direction; as your opponent takes a step forward and punches with his left hand toward your head, deflect his punch with your right hand (Figure 49). If you can strike Lung 5, Lung 5a, Lung 6, Lung 6a, or Lung 9 on your opponents left arm with your right hand, this could set up a "vestibular postural reflex." Your opponent's reaction would be to move his left leg forward to regain his balance and relieve a moment of tension in his neck. As your opponent continues his attack and punches toward your face with his right hand, use your left forearm to deflect his punch away from your face (Figure 50).

49

50

At the same time, slide your left forearm over the top of his right hand and then use your left palm heel to strike Small Intestine 17 (Figure 53). Or, if your opponent turns his head sufficiently you could be striking Gallbladder 20. Gallbladder 20 (Figure 52) is located at the back of the head in a slight depression. This is the occipital foramen, where two major nerves are located, the greater and lesser occipital nerves. If you strike these points in and slightly upward, you will be able to knock out your opponent. This location is where a "rabbit punch" is delivered. Please refer to the discussion of the rabbit punch in Chapter 2. It goes without saying that striking this point with any degree of force could prove extremely dangerous to your opponent, so restraint is necessary when practicing this technique.

Small Intestine 17 (Figure 53) is located posterior to the angle of the mandible (jaw) on the border of the medial sternocleidomastoid muscle.

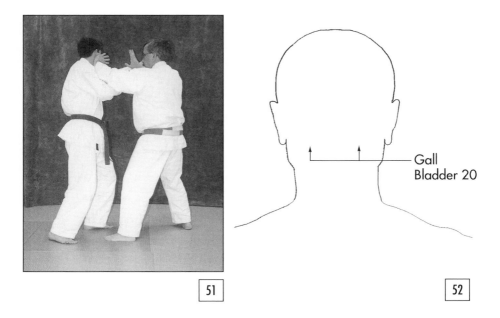

Gall Bladder 20

51

52

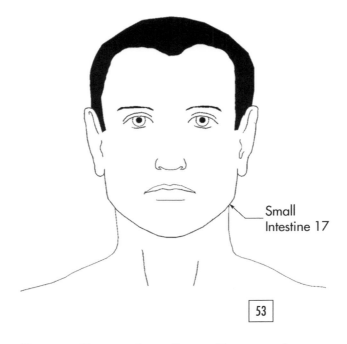

Small
Intestine 17

53

PINAN - HEIAN - PYUNG AHN 4 — DEFENSE AGAINST A PUNCH TO THE HEAD 2

In the following sequence, your opponent reaches out with his right hand (Figure 54). Begin to deflect his right arm with your left hand and bring your right hand up and under his wrist (Figure 55). Grab just above your opponent's elbow and press Heart 3 with your left thumb. Heart 3 is located just above the elbow joint on the indentation next to the tendon on the inside of the upper arm (Figure 56). In most cases, your opponent will react by lifting his arm and pulling back slightly from you. When he does this, grab his fingers with your right hand (Figure 57), a close up view of this is seen in Figure 60. Remember when you use this lock your thumb should be pressed firmly against the base of the forefinger, and use your index and middle finger to press the little finger of your opponent behind his fingers. Continue pressure on your opponent's right fingers and wrist by bringing your right hand down to your center; maintain pressure with your left thumb on Heart 3 (Figure 59). Press your opponent's arm down with your left hand and cross his wrist over your left arm (Figure 58). Please note that, for clarity, the view on Figures 57 and 58 have been rotated.

54

55

56

57

58

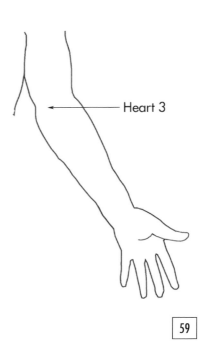

Heart 3

59

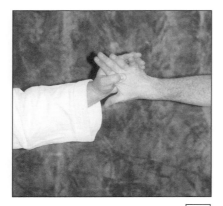

60

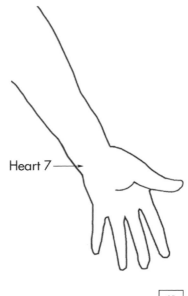

Heart 7

61

When grabbing the wrist as in Figure 56, it may be possible to apply pressure to Heart 7 with the base of your index finger. Heart 7 can be located by having your training partner make a tight fist and flex the hand inward. The point will be located in the crease of the arm and slightly to the inside of the ulna.

PINAN 4 — DEFENSE AGAINST A PUNCH TO THE HEAD 3

Continuing on the theme of target selection and the use of the initial movements of Pinan 4, your opponent faces you and prepares to initiate an attack. Your hands have not yet come to a defensive posture (Figure 62); make use of the instinctive reflex to raise your hands to protect your face and deflect your opponent's right hand with your left hand (Figure 63). Shift your body weight forward slightly as you turn toward your left, and strike Lung 1 and 2 (Figure 66).

Lung 1 is located on the front of the body, two inches from the nipple (in the direction of the arm) and up three ribs. The point is between the first

62 63

64   65

and second ribs from the top. Lung 2 is found approximately 6 inches lateral to the midline of the chest and at the level of the lower border of the clavicle. You can find this point by flexing your upper body; the point will then be in a depression in the infraclavicular fossa. Figure 66 shows you the location of these points.

There were several concepts covered with the bunkai examples from Pinan 4:

1. Individual movements in kata may offer you self-defense techniques from both the front and rear. When you begin to analyze your own kata it is important not to be "stuck" and see attacks only from the front. By keeping your mind open and thinking creatively, you may be able to discover excellent self-defense techniques from the rear.

2. In self-defense situations, by having a good grasp of multiple points you will be able to attack "targets of opportunity." In real-life it is highly unlikely that you will be presented with an attack exactly as you have practiced it in the dojo. You must be able to modify your

techniques rapidly and select targets to strike on your opponent without conscious thought. By drilling in specific techniques that have multiple targets, you should be able to increase your response to a particular type of attack.

3. By using the same repetitive defensive technique, you increase the probability that your hands and body will move in a particular way. As you have seen, the physical movement of your hands and body mimics that of the two movements in Pinan 4. However the techniques are varied and offer the range of defensive techniques. You may have noticed in these techniques that my right hand was forward as in the kata. Further, when I needed to take a step forward, I did so with my left leg, again, as in the kata. My opponent attacked with both right and left hands, yet my right hand continued to stay in the forward position.

You should be able to integrate these three principles into other applications in your kata. As stated earlier, I have no idea if any of these techniques were used by the creators of this movement. To me that is not relevant. If I feel that any one of these techniques would be useful for me in a self-defense situation, then the utility of practicing this movement becomes self-evident. If you find any other techniques I've described useful, or if you have your own particular bunkai you feel is correct, then no one should be able to tell you what you're doing is incorrect. The value of kata lies in the ability of the individual to practice techniques they would use in a self-defense situation. There is no value for the individual to practice bunkai their teacher would use in self-defense.

We should remember that kata were designed by individuals who depended on their skill in the martial arts to stay alive. When that person practiced his kata, it was for his benefit; each movement was practiced as if he were in an actual combat situation. These masters intuitively understood a sound principle of psychology; individuals revert to previously learned behavior in moments of stress. By practicing technique over and over, you build what some call "muscle memory."

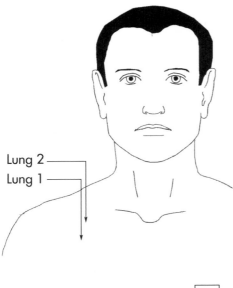

Lung 2
Lung 1

66

67

NAIHANCHI 2 (TEKKI/CHULGI)

Naihanchi 2 is a kata that has been practiced in Japanese, Okinawan, and Korean karate. In the following section, there will be a number of examples of bunkai from this form. Rather than illustrate this kata in its entirety I've chosen to illustrate three sections of it. The movements in kata may vary slightly from system to system, but the general format should be relatively consistent. This form, like Naihanchi 1, can be performed as a mirror image. In the following pictures the kata is performed starting to the right side first. It is possible to do exactly the same movements in the form starting to the left. From the ready position (Figure 67), step across your right foot with your left and bring your arms level with your breast (Figure 68). Step to your right side with your right leg, position your left hand in front of your solar plexus, and strike at neck height with your right hammer fist (Figure 69). Continue moving toward your right side by crossing your left leg behind your right, bring your right fist in a circular motion past your face, and bring

68

69

70

71

your left fist under your right elbow (Figure 70). The last movement in the sequence (Figure 71) is similar to Figure 69.

The kata repeats this sequence of movements, and the next major sequence of movements is illustrated in the following four figures. Your right fist is at face height with your palm facing up. Your left knife hand is resting alongside the wrist of your right hand (Figure 72). You pull your right hand back to your waist and cover your fist with your left knife hand (Figure 73).

Sharply raise your right knee in front of you and keep your hands back toward your waist (Figure 74). As your foot touches the ground, strike across your body with your right elbow and maintain contact with your left hand on your right fist (Figure 75).

The third and final sequence from Naihanchi 2, you'll find in other kata. For example, the same sequence of movements is found in Naihanchi 1 and 3. You'll also find similar movements in other kata such as Pinan 3.

In the initial movement, there is an inside block with the left hand (Figure 76). Your right hand moves down in front of your groin (Figure 77),

72

73

74

75

76

77

and immediately you change your hand position with a circular motion, so that your right fist comes up and your left fist is down (Figure 78). Your right hand executes an uppercut punch at the same time that your left fist comes under your right elbow (Figure 79).

78

79

80

NAIHANCHI 2 - LAPEL GRAB 1

As with any sequence of techniques in kata, there can be multiple applications. I strongly believe these applications are limited only by the imagination of the practitioner and by his or her previous experience in various martial arts. In the first example, attack is initiated by your opponent grabbing your left lapel with his right hand (Figure 80). Immediately strike Pericardium 7 with your right fist; you should slightly pull your right fist toward your body as you make contact with this point (Figure 81). Your left fist should strike on the back of your opponent's forearm directly opposite your right fist. While there are vital points in this area, your left hand serves primarily as an "anvil," so that when you strike with your right fist, your opponent's arm is in a secure position. Another reason to place your fist on the back of your opponents hand is to give you a landmark. Most people have no problem in touching their fingertips to each other without looking, your body sends messages to your brain to help you orient your movements.

81   82

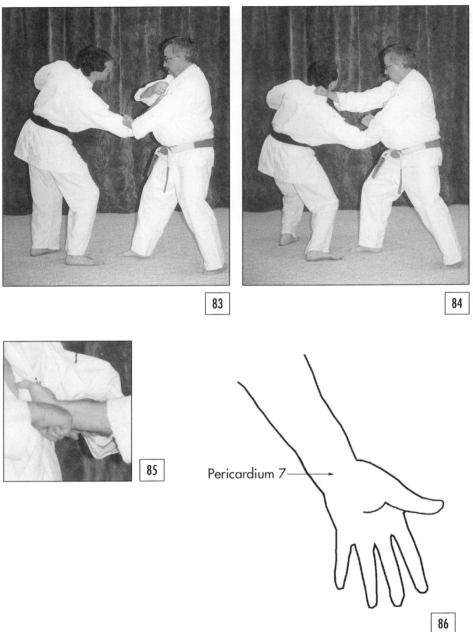

Pericardium 7

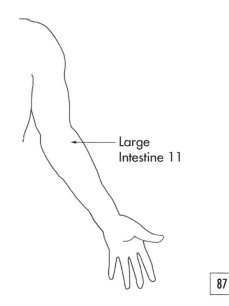

Large
Intestine 11

87

Pericardium 7 (Figure 86) is found at the transverse crease of the wrist between the tendons. Initially this can be a difficult point to strike; however, with practice, you should be able to strike this point with a high degree of accuracy. When striking this point, the typical reaction will be a numbing of the hand, and it will cause your opponent to bend forward and turn his head to the side. You will also notice that your opponent's opposite hand will tend to move away from you, and his front knee will buckle. I have, on occasion, been able to cause an opponent to become light-headed. It is possible with some individuals to knock them out using this point. It is not a point that gives you a high probability of a knock out, but it will give you a strong reaction with the majority of individuals.

A close up view (Figure 85) shows the position of your fist when striking this point. While it is possible to strike this point with your palm facing your own body I've had the best success with the palm facing the floor.

Once your opponent's legs begin to buckle, it's possible to strike Large Intestine 11 with your left hammer fist (Figures 83 and 87). If you strike this point at a 45-degree angle down and toward the fingertips, you should be able to numb your opponent's lower arm. You will also cause your opponent to turn his body away from the strike. So, if you strike from left to right, your opponent will turn toward his left. This opens up targets on the back of the neck. As you can see, Gallbladder 20 becomes a "target of opportunity" (Figure 84). This combination of strikes will give you a high percentage of knockouts. Anytime you are striking the head or neck, there is a potential for serious damage to your opponent. Great care must be exercised with such techniques. In practice you should never strike these points hard—only very light contact should be made.

NAIHANCHI 2 — DOUBLE WRIST GRAB

In this sequence of techniques your opponent has initiated the attack by grabbing both of your wrists (Figure 88). This is the ready position at the beginning of Naihanchi 2. Bring both of your hands up toward your upper chest and rotate your palms so that they face toward your body. This will have the effect of loosening your opponent's grip. As you pull your fists together grab his left wrist with your right hand. You need not remove your left wrist from his grasp to accomplish this movement (Figure 89).

88   89

At this point, push your right elbow forward and pull your wrist free from your opponent's grasp. Do not pull your wrist completely away from your opponent but maintain a slight degree of contact. As you pull out, you press your forearm against your opponent's fingers and counter rotate his wrist (Figure 90). It is possible to grab Heart 7 (Figure 61) with your left thumb (Figure 91). When you press on Heart 7, be sure to use the side of your thumb. This allows you to use a bony portion of your thumb to apply pressure. If you use the pad of your thumb, you will not be able to elicit the same degree of pain (Figure 94).

90   91

When you counterrotate your opponent's wrist, try to get his little finger to go behind his ring finger. This will increase the amount of pressure he feels on his wrist (Figure 93).

As this wrist lock is applied, you have control over your opponent's left wrist, and most likely he will continue to hold your left wrist with his right hand. This gives you one free hand with which to counterattack (Figure 91). In this instance, Triple Warmer 17 (Figure 94) is open. In other scenarios, points other than Triple Warmer 17 may present themselves; if so, do not hesitate to attack any vital point you are familiar with.

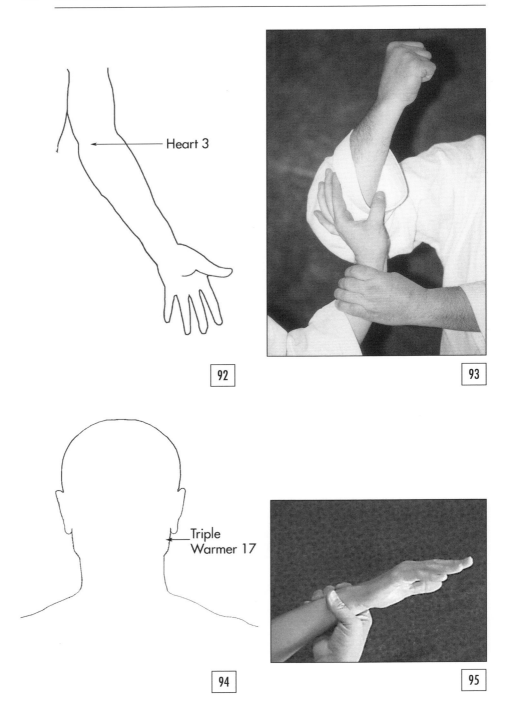

Heart 3

92

93

Triple
Warmer 17

94

95

NAIHANCHI 2 — CROSS-HAND WRIST GRAB

In the neck sequence of movements referred to in Figures 69, 70, and 71 from Naihanchi 2, your opponent attacks with a cross-hand grab to your left wrist. Re-grab his wrist with your left hand; if possible apply pressure to Lung 9 with the side of your left thumb (Figures 96 and 100). Turn your body toward your opponent so that you can strike Large Intestine 14 with the tip of your right elbow (Figure 97). This will cause your opponent to move away from you; his knees will buckle, and then he will feel a numbing sensation in his arm. Large Intestine 14 (Figure 103) is found approximately one inch up from the tip of the deltoid muscle. It is at the edge of the deltoid muscle in a small depression. If you run your finger along this muscle, you can feel a slight "valley" where this point is located.

96   97

Allow your arm to follow through and pass over your opponent's arm (Figure 98). Once your arm has passed across your opponent's arm. strike back on Triple Warmer 13 with the tip of your right elbow. Triple Warmer 13 is located directly opposite of Large Intestine 14. When you strike this point with your right elbow, you'll notice your opponent's knees buckle and his head will probably turn toward his left. This offers you multiple targets of opportunity. If his head does turn sharply toward the left, Stomach 9 (Figure 101) presents itself as a good target to strike with your hammer fist or your forearm. If his head does not rotate as much, you may find Triple Warmer 17 to be an excellent target (Figure 104). Either of these two points can knock your opponent out.

98

99

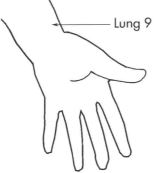

Lung 9

100

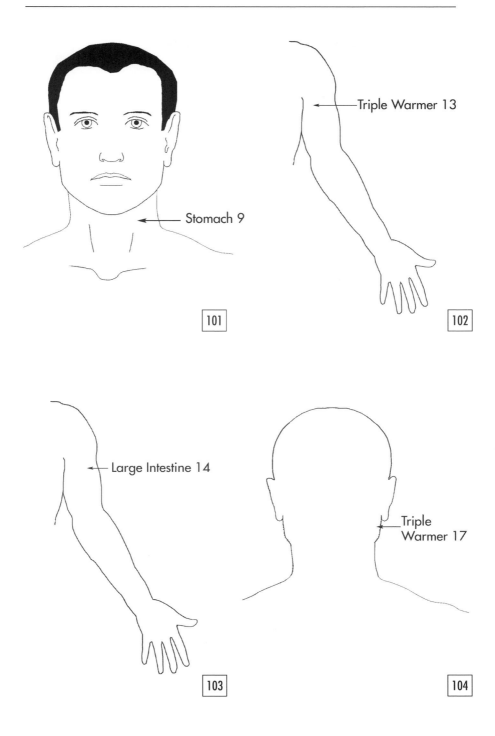

Stomach 9

Triple Warmer 13

101

102

Large Intestine 14

Triple Warmer 17

103

104

105   106

NAIHANCHI 2 — SAME-SIDE ARM GRAB

In this sequence we'll be looking at two movements found in Naihanchi 2 (Figures105 and 106). This inside blocking motion could be used for a joint lock. In this situation, your opponent attacks with a same-side grip slightly above your elbow (Figure 107).

Immediately grab your opponent's fingers with your left hand, and swing your right forearm across your body to lock his wrist in place (Figure 108). If possible, try to get your fingers underneath your opponent's and lift his little finger up and over the back of his fingers as you execute this technique (Figure 109). For a close up of this, look at Figure 110. Notice that this lock is similar to other techniques demonstrated throughout this book.

You can continue pressure on your opponent's wrist to take him to the ground, or you may find him in a position to kick a vital point.

107

108

109

110

111

112

113

114

NAIHANCHI 2 — SAME-SIDE WRIST GRAB

This technique can be seen in the movements of Naihanchi 2 (Figures 74 and 75). In this technique, an opponent is being verbally aggressive, and the potential for physical confrontation is present. Sometimes if you extend your arm, an opponent will grab your wrist. So extend your arm toward your opponent with your hand about shoulder height, if your opponent grabs your wrist, he will probably grab it with his thumb up (Figure 111).

As your opponent grabs your wrist, push your elbow forward with a slight turn of your body; this will facilitate pulling your wrist back into your body and extending your opponent's arm. At the same time you're performing this action, you grab his wrist to eliminate the possibility of your opponent's withdrawing his arm (Figure 112).

As you turn your body, execute a front kick to his leg to disrupt his balance. You could kick Stomach 34 on the outside of his leg (Figure 113). This point is located in the muscle that runs on the outside of the thigh, two inches up from the kneecap (Figure 115). If your opponent has his right leg forward, you could target Spleen 10 (Figure 116). This point is in the same general location as Stomach 34, but on the inside of the leg. An easy way to find this point is to have your training partner sit and bend his or her leg at a 90-degree angle. Place the center of your palm on the center of his or her kneecap; your thumb will touch Spleen 9 two inches above the kneecap on the inside of the leg.

Complete this technique by applying an arm bar to your opponent. There are several considerations in performing and effective arm bar. As with any joint lock, you want to make sure that all slack is removed from the appendage you are locking prior to applying force on the joint. If you plan to snap a twig that is not perfectly dry, there will be a certain degree of bend before you reach the point at which it snaps. Your opponent's joints are similar in that you cannot break them until you have reached the point where they no longer have any movement. Therefore to gain maximum pain compliance or to break the joint, you must first take up the slack.

You also need to be certain that you are using your body weight to maximum advantage. With this arm bar, once you have locked the opponent's arm to your body, you can use body shifting to apply pressure to the joint. There are two points you can use to lock your opponent's arm to your body. The first, and most obvious, is at your opponent's wrist. Be sure to use both of your hands to grip your opponent's wrist. If possible, attempt to apply pressure with either your fingertips or the side edge of your thumb to one of the vital points located at the wrist. The second point of contact with your opponent will be your chest and upper arm. You want to have your arm slightly above your opponent's elbow, as illustrated in Figure 115. Pressure to your opponent's arm should be applied by pulling your elbow tight into your body and pushing up at your opponent's wrist. To insure effective pain compliance, your opponent's elbow should be pointed directly at the ceiling. If your opponent's elbow is covered with clothing, it may be difficult to gauge the direction of the elbow. However, there is a simple solution to this problem. You need only ensure that your opponent has his palm facing your

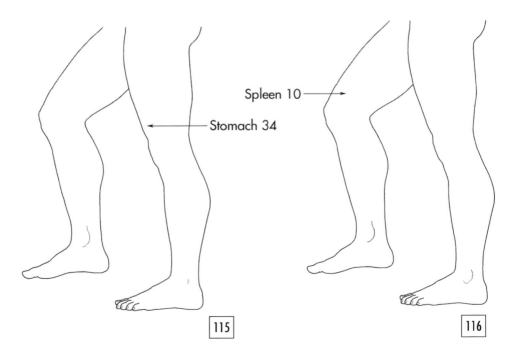

Spleen 10

Stomach 34

115   116

body and that his little finger is facing the ceiling. This will place his elbow in the appropriate position to apply pressure directly down.

To apply this pressure, you need only assume a "horse stance" and drop your body weight straight down. This will apply force directly down on your opponent's arm and cause him to drop toward the ground. A common mistake that individuals make when applying this lock is to bend their upper body forward in an attempt to increase pressure on the joint. If you stop and look at the dynamics of this action, it is clear that pressure is actually lessened rather than increased. Consider that as you bend your body forward, your arms must follow your body movement. And as you bend forward, your opponent's wrist will be turned so that the palm is facing more toward the ceiling. Then as you press down, the pressure is no longer directly against the joint, but at a slight angle. This can allow your opponent to turn out of the joint lock. It is imperative that pressure be exerted directly on the joint to cause maximum pain compliance or possibly break the joint.

NAIHANCHI 2 — LAPEL GRAB 1

Naihanchi 1, 2, and 3 overlap several hand actions (see Figures 76, 77, 78, and 79). One possible application for this section involves your opponent grabbing your lapel (Figure 117). If your opponent is grabbing your shoulder, upper arm, or lapel, invariably it will be a same-side grab, his right hand grabbing the left side of your body. It is highly unlikely that he would grab with a cross-handed grab, his right hand grabbing your right shoulder, elbow, or lapel. If the opponent were to grab in a cross-handed fashion, it would place him in a vulnerable position. His arm would be extended and his elbow placed in a position where it could be locked with little effort. In addition, his free hand would be farther away from your body, making it more difficult to effectively punch.

Use your left forearm to create an "anvil" by striking your opponent's arm in and toward your body. At the same time strike Heart 2 (Figure 121) with your right foreknuckles (Figure 118). This strike should be up and into the bone. This will cause an intense amount of pain if struck correctly, as well as a numbing sensation in the arm.

117

118

Your opponent should release the grip on your lapel with this strike. Your left forearm can be used to guide the opponent's arm down, as your right hand guides his arm up (Figure 119). As you guide the opponent's arm, shift your body position toward the left or back of your opponent. Begin to pull your opponent into your body at this time. This combination of movements will turn your opponent and position you behind him.

By continuing to circle your left hand around, you can grab your opponent slightly above the elbow and lock him in position (Figure 120). Pressure can be applied to this lock by pressing down with your left palm and lifting your left elbow.

At this point you could work techniques that would elicit pain compliance from your opponent. If you were to continue the motion found in the kata, you would be delivering an uppercut punch with your right hand (Figure 120). Depending on the position of your opponent, you may have a variety of points open to attack. In this instance, Gallbladder 20 presents itself as a viable target of opportunity (Figure 122).

119   120

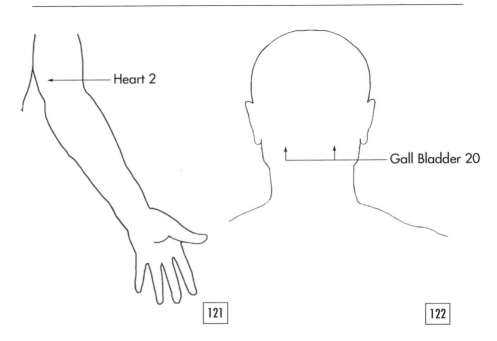

Heart 2

Gall Bladder 20

121

122

NAIHANCHI 2 — LAPEL GRAB 2

To continue with alternate explanations for the movements in the Naihanchi kata (Figures 76, 77, 78, and 79), your opponent again has grabbed your lapel with a same-side grab (Figure 123). If your opponent immediately strikes at you with his right hand, you must immediately block your opponent's punch. I do not like to look at this movement so much as a block, but rather as a deflection of the opponent's attack. As his right hand comes at your head, turn your body slightly to the side and begin to circle your left hand to intercept your opponent's punch (Figure 124).

At this point, you will have made contact with your opponent's wrist and will be directing his arm down and toward your waist (Figure 125). Your right hand will be punching your opponent's central line down and at a 45-degree angle (Figure 126). The size of your opponent in relationship to your own size will determine an appropriate target to attack. Virtually any punch directed at the center line will cause your opponent a great deal of discomfort.

123

124

125

126

In this illustration (Figure 126), the back of the forearm is being used to strike Large Intestine 17 (Figure 127). This point is located on the posterior border of the sternocleidomastoid muscle. The strike to this point can cause a knockout, numbing of the arm, and a tingling sensation down to the foot. This is an extremely effective point to use in self-defense (Figure 5).

While striking Large Intestine 17, Stomach 9 could also be an extremely effective target of opportunity, if Large Intestine was not available. Depending on the reaction of your opponent, points might become available on the head or neck. You may find points available on the upper arm, such as Large Intestine 14.

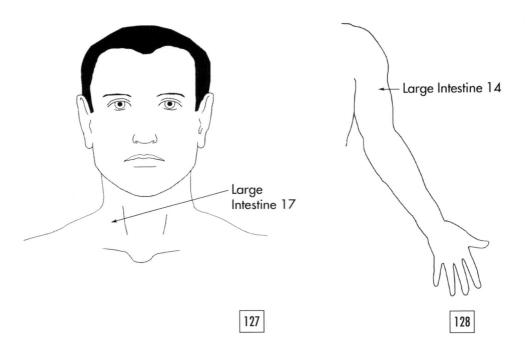

Large Intestine 14

Large Intestine 17

127

128

THROWS
Throwing Applications Found in Kata — Lunge Punch

It has become obvious that when we are looking at typical techniques that many consider to be blocks, alternate explanations give us striking, throwing, and joint-locking techniques. If we can look at blocks as strikes, we might also view our striking and kicking techniques as something more. To give a simple example: the lunge punch (Figure 129) is a technique found in almost every system of martial arts. This technique in kata is repeated numerous times and is of obvious value to the martial artist. I would like to do a little out-of-the-box thinking with this punch. Could there be an alternate explanation for a simple punch? In other words, could we make use of this motion in a way other than the obvious punch to your opponent? With a simple example, I think the answer is quite apparent. To me it is very important to look at each and every technique in kata and attempt to look past the obvious explanation. I want to expand the possible explanations for every move in kata.

129 130

In this example your opponent has grabbed your left wrist with his left hand. Rotate your hand in a clockwise manner so that your thumb presses on Lung 9 (Figures 130 and 134). As you press on this point, begin to pull your opponent's arm back to your waist (Figure 131). You should turn his arm in such away that his palm is facing directly away from your body, and your upper arm is slightly above his elbow. This will place you in a position where you can apply pressure to the elbow joint of your opponent as you step forward and punch (Figure. 132).

As you step forward, you'll find that your opponent will move up to the tips of his toes, and his balance will be broken in forward direction. This will give you the option of continuing your forward motion and throwing your opponent (Figure 133).

If your opponent is not thrown with this technique, you do have the possibility of dislocating his elbow. When you do this technique, there are several key points to remember. You cannot generate the force needed for this technique using only your arm strength. You must use the forward momentum of your body in conjunction with your hands to generate sufficient force to throw your opponent or dislocate his elbow.

131   132

133

134

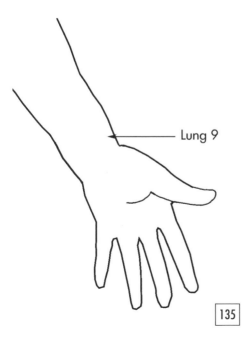

 Lung 9

135

Throwing Applications in Kata — Side Kick - Uchimata

Sometimes when you look at kata, the techniques just don't seem to make sense. For example, many kata have a side kick or front kick in which you stand on one leg with your hands pulled to your waist (Figures 136 and 137). The problem I have with this technique comes from years of sparring practice. I don't think I can ever remember a time when I would have had my hands in such a position prior to executing a side kick. Invariably you would have your hands in front of your body guarding against your opponent's punches or kicks. It is just not sensible to have your hands in such a defenseless position, unless you were doing something with your hands that required them to be in such a position. Now, why would you have your hands pulled back to your waist? Clearly your hands are not in a position to be blocking any type of attack by an opponent. Your hands do not enhance your balance in such a position. It is only logical therefore that your hands must be in contact with your opponent. The two most likely points of contact would be with either her arm or leg.

136   137

If we make the assumption that our opponent has grabbed our wrist, we can begin to develop a technique utilizing this common technique from kata. In this scenario your left wrist is grabbed with your opponent's left hand (Figure 138).

Immediately turn your body toward your right and begin the application of *nikyo*, or an "s" lock (Figure 139). This will begin to cause your opponent to lose his balance and diminish his ability to punch or kick you. Once your opponent has begun to lose his balance in a forward direction, hold his arm to your left side and sharply raise your right leg. This motion is somewhat similar to "chambering" a sidekick. It might be possible at this time to deliver a knee kick to your opponent's chin (Figure 140).

Once your opponent's balance has been broken, strongly thrust your leg between your opponent's legs. The point of contact should be your upper thigh to his inner thigh. Exert pressure with your right arm behind his elbow to force his weight over the little toe of his right leg (Figure 141).

138   139

Once your opponent's balance is completely broken, continue the motion of your right leg to further unbalance your opponent. Your left hand should be pulling your opponent's left arm toward your waist, and your right arm pushing your opponent's weight over his left toe (Figure 142).

140

141

142

This will give you a throw similar to the *uchimata,* inner thigh throw, found in judo. This throw is an extremely popular throw for tournament competitors in judo because of its effectiveness.

Once again what I'm trying to illustrate is that techniques may have multiple bunkai, and when there is a technique that appears obvious, there may be more subtle explanations for it. As stated earlier, with this movement the two most likely points of contact would be either the arm or leg of your opponent. In this instance, the technique involved your opponent's arm.

Throwing Applications in Kata — Side Kick - Leg Takedown

In this bunkai for a side kick in kata I would like to look at the possible explanation that your opponent's leg is the point of contact with your hands. Your opponent initiates a sidekick with their right leg (Figures 143 and 144); as he does so, prepare to shift your weight to your rear leg and begin to block his right leg with your hands. Once contact has been made with his leg, grip firmly at the ankle and place your right hand around the knee (Figure 145).

143   144

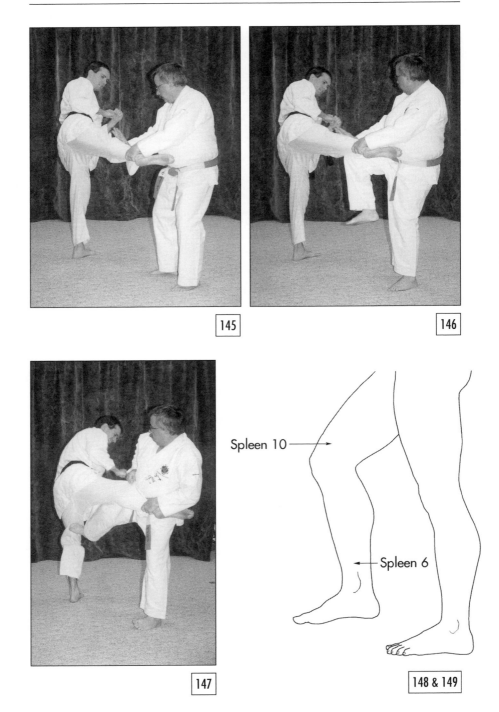

145

146

147

Spleen 10

Spleen 6

148 & 149

Immediately chamber your side kick, so that in effect this action can be used to knee Spleen 6 (Figure 146).

Once you have delivered a knee kick to this point, immediately kick the back of your opponent's Knee, Bladder 40, to disrupt his balance (Figure 146). Or, if other points, such as Spleen 10, present themselves as a target of opportunity, it would be appropriate to deliver a kick to that area.

Spleen 6 (Figure 149) can be found by placing your hand on the inside of your partner's leg. If you rest your fingers on the top of the ankle bone, this point will be forcing your fingers up and behind the shin bone. This point is highly sensitive and can cause a great deal of pain in most people. It is even possible to knock some people out with a strike to this point.

Side Kick Application from Grappling Distance

This technique is very similar to the previous technique. However, in this sequence, you are at grappling distance from your opponent. He may have grabbed your upper-left shoulder in preparation for a throw or to punch you. Your response would be to grab his right shoulder and have your right forearm in a position to defend against a punch if needed (Figure 150). With your right knee, kick Spleen 10 or any other target of opportunity to get your opponent to raise his right leg from the ground (Figure 151). With his right leg off the ground, all of his weight will be placed on his left knee. Side kick Spleen 10, or even any place above the knee, (Figure 152) to disrupt his balance (Figure 153). It would be optimal to kick down on Spleen 10 in this technique. It is possible to have your opponent's leg locked into a position that, as you deliver your side kick, you would break his leg, dislocate the knee, or tear tendons and ligaments. So this is a technique that should be practiced with due care.

Remember, when you're looking at kicks in kata, to have an open mind. Perhaps a kata you perform uses a front kick or a roundhouse kick rather than the side kick illustrated in this technique. It would still be possible to use the basic concept of this technique—so you might modify it to fit your particular system or style. Also, remember that your opponent could kick with a front kick or roundhouse kick, and you could still execute the same technique.

Throwing Applications in Kata — Bassai - Taiotoshi

This movement out of *bassai* (Figure 154) is one of those movements that appears to have limited practical application. A basic bunkai sometimes offered is: the right arm is to block an oncoming low-level punch or kick. While it may be possible to execute such a technique, it does not seem to be one that would offer a great deal of strength. If you were to assume this stance, it would take very little effort for someone to push you off-balance in the direction of your left shoulder. Again the question needs to be asked is there an alternate explanation for this movement in the kata?

Cross-training in various martial arts offers you the ability to visualize techniques from other systems. I think it's important to remember that in the old days martial arts were not as specialized as we tend to make them today. Martial artists would have been familiar with throwing techniques, grappling techniques, and percussive techniques. So if we're to explore bunkai to its fullest extent, we must be willing to look at techniques that may be found

150   151

152

153

154

in other systems such as judo, jujitsu, or aikido. The position in this kata is reminiscent of the judo throw *tai-otoshi*, body drop.

Your opponent grabs your left wrist with his right hand and prepares to punch with his left hand (Figure 155). When he punches toward your face with his left hand, turn your body toward your right and deflect his punch with your right hand. At the same time re-grab the his right hand with your left hand (Figure 156). Begin to pull your opponent to his right-front corner. Attempt to grip his arm slightly above the elbow with your right hand and push his elbow in the direction of his right little toe.

Step across his right leg with your right leg, so that your calf is below his knee, and the back of your calf is just above his ankle. Pull his right arm across your chest and down toward your waist. Your right hand should continue pushing your opponent over his little toe (Figure 157).

Continue turning your body in a counterclockwise motion, and throw your opponent over your right leg (Figure 158).

In practice, you should take care to make sure that your leg is never above your opponent's knee. If this should happen and you do throw your opponent, you have a very real possibility of severely injuring his or her knee.

155

156

157   158

Throwing Applications in Kata — Jitte - Shipsu - Osotogari

This movement out of the *kata Jitte*, or *Shipsu* from the Korean systems, (Figures 159, 160, and 161) is an interesting move. If you tend to think only in terms of karate or tae kwon do, there does not seem to be much logic in such awkward hand position and leg movement. If you step outside of your normal thought process and consider the possibility that this movement could be from a grappling system, then it may begin to make sense.

With your hands in such a high position, there are several things I would like you to consider. First is the fact that in the original form the hands may not have been held as high, and may have been more in line with the shoulder area. Also, with both hands in such a position, it would seem likely that your points of contact with your opponent would be rather far apart. As an example, you might be grabbing at your opponent's wrist and on the opposite side of his body at the same time. This gives the feeling of stretching your opponent in some manner. If you have your opponent stretched out, it seems likely that he would be unbalanced in one direction or the other. Therefore, a throwing technique would seem to be a logical path to explore. Judo offers a technique known as *osotogari* (major outer reaping throw).

As your opponent attacks with his right hand, deflect the oncoming motion with your left hand (Figure 162). At the same time, turn your body toward his and strike the side of his head or neck with your forearm or hammer fist. When you make the strike, there are number of vital points suitable for attack such as Stomach 9 or Triple Warmer 17 (Figures 166 and 167). Of course other points, should they be available to attack, would be equally effective. The intent of the strike is to disrupt the balance of your opponent or possibly knock him out.

Once your opponent's balance has been broken, use your right leg to throw your opponent. Your right hand can continue its force, pushing your opponent toward his right-rear corner, and your left hand can pull away from his body (Figure 163). It is critical that your opponent's weight be shifted toward his right heel for this throw. Bring your right leg behind your opponent's right leg (Figure 164) and sweep his right leg. This should throw your opponent in front of you (Figure 165). As with any technique, it is important to move your entire body as one unit rather than make individual motions. This will greatly increase the strength of your technique.

Some throwing techniques in kata can provide useful follow-up techniques once the person has been thrown. I speculate that there are some techniques in kata that are designed to be used as a grappling technique, only practiced in a standing position. If you are familiar with judo or jujutsu, you can see from the last picture that you would be in a good position to execute a *juji gatame* (arm bar). In the next series of movements, there will be some examples of movements that could be used on the ground.

159

160

161

162

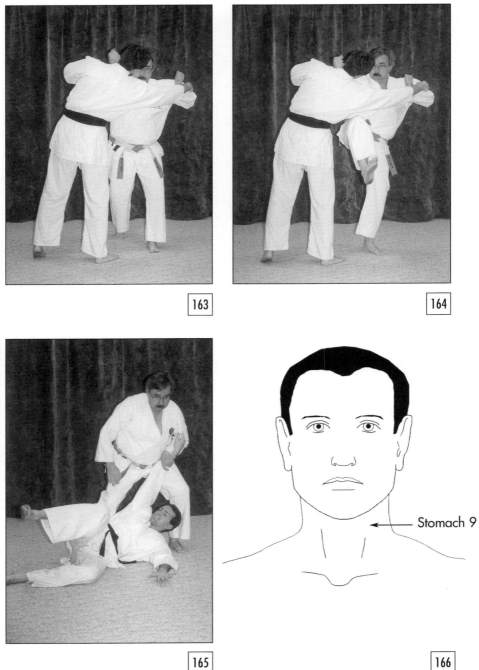

163

164

165

166

Stomach 9

Throwing Applications to Grappling Techniques in Kata — Empi - Sankakujime

In this section, I would like to advance a somewhat controversial proposition. If we accept that traditional kata were designed for practice in self-defense applications, every move in kata should contain effective self-defense techniques. Techniques would not be included in the kata to give esthetic beauty as might be expected today from kata competition. Given that movements in kata are designed for self-defense, we need to look at some common requirements of any effective technique. To deliver a well-focused punch or kick, we must be in a position that affords us balance and stability. Any technique that we attempt to perform from an unbalanced or unstable position will not allow us to generate the appropriate amount of force required to be effective.

When we look at various movements in kata, we can readily identify techniques that give you an inherently balanced and stable position. It is patently obvious these techniques could be delivered with enough force to be effective. Equally obvious are sections of the various kata that are intrinsically unstable and unbalanced. This flies in the face of our basic assumptions. Therefore, any technique that does not meet our criterion for balance and stability either must not be an effective self-defense technique or our way of viewing the technique is flawed. I propose that the latter is more likely true. This offers us a perfect opportunity to employ some out-of-the-box thinking. If the view we have of a technique indicates an inherently unstable or unbalanced posture, we must ask "is there an angle or view that we could use that would change the unbalanced stance to a balanced stance, or the unstable stance to a stable stance?"

Looking at a kata common to a number of systems, *Empi/Eunbi*, I would like to offer a possible answer to this question. I will be looking at one sequence found in this kata that consists of a stance where you're balanced on one leg and your other leg is tucked behind your knee. This brief sequence starts with your right hand at your belt and your left knife hand covering your fist (Figure 168). You then deliver a knife hand strike with your left hand (Figure 169). Once you have executed the knife hand strike, you bring

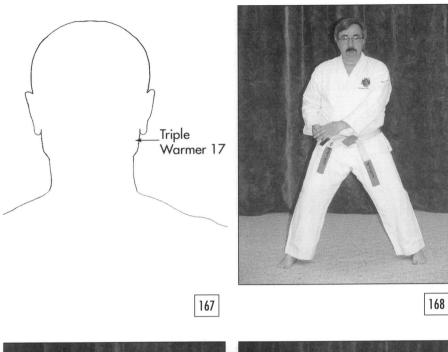

Triple
Warmer 17

167

168

169

170

your right forearm to your left hand, and your right leg comes behind your left knee (Figure 170). This stance, quite obviously, is not a stable or balanced position. There is one way in which your body position in Figure 170 could be extremely balanced and stable. To see this, you must step outside of the box and visualize other dimensions. In this case to achieve a very balanced and stable position you simply have to lie on your back.

For this sequence of moves, your opponent is attacking your face by punching with their right hand. Deflect his hand to the side with your left hand (Figure 171). Guide your opponent's punch toward your right side so you can grab his wrist with your right hand. Allow your left hand to continue in the direction it was traveling and apply pressure to your opponent's elbow with your left forearm (Figure 172). This will cause your opponent's balance to be broken to their front-right corner.

Strike Large Intestine 14 with your left elbow to cause your opponent's balance to collapse and to pull his weight onto his right leg (Figure 172). This position will set up your opponent for a throw.

171   172

Use your forearm to strike against your opponent's face and turn his head toward his left shoulder. If you continue rotating his head and pull your arm back toward your left, you can throw your opponent (Figure 173).

Once your opponent has landed on the ground pull his arm up sharply (Figure 174). Slide your right foot in over the front of your opponent and hook your ankle just below his left ear. As you're doing this, squat as close as you can to his upper body while extending his left arm (Figure 175) and drop to the ground, keeping his arm as close to your groin as possible (Figure 176).

At this point, lock your right instep behind your left knee (Figure 177); your leg position will be exactly as in Figure 178. Your hands will continue their grip on your opponent's wrist. If you continue stretching his arm and pull his arm down and toward your chest, at the same time raising your hips, you will be performing an arm bar similar to juji gatame. Your leg position will allow you to choke your opponent by applying pressure to the side of his neck; this position is similar to sankakujime.

173

174

As you can see, the body position of this grappling technique is the same as in the kata. The only difference is the orientation of the technique; rather than being a standing technique this was done as a grappling maneuver. Undoubtedly the technique performed as a grappling maneuver will have a greater degree of stability and balance than it would as a technique executed from a standing position on one leg. This may or may not have been the original bunkai for this technique. To my mind it really does not matter if this was be part of the original bunkai. This explanation offers, for me, a logical and practical application for this movement in the kata. When practicing this movement in the kata, I can visualize myself utilizing this technique. Therefore, no matter what anyone tells me, I'm able to practice this technique in my kata. I am strongly convinced that if I were to be placed in a situation in which this technique could be used, I would have the ability to execute this movement without conscious thought.

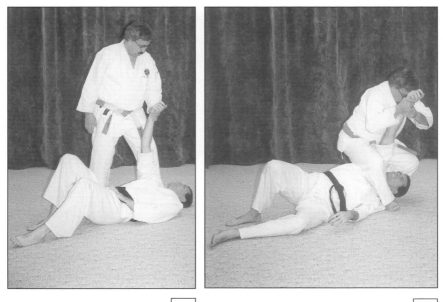

175   176

177

178

THROWING TO GRAPPLING

Throwing Applications to Grappling Techniques in Kata - Pinan 5 — Standing Arm Bar Using Your Leg

Pinan 5 is a kata that contains many interesting combinations of techniques. One such group of techniques has an open hand strike with your left hand (Figure 178) followed immediately by a crescent kick and low block (Figures 179, 180, and 181). This low block performed with your hand closed could be perceived as a strike with a hammer fist.

One of the things I like to do when analyzing kata is to say to myself "what if a kick is not a kick or a punch is not punch or a block is not a block." Then I like to construct applications that make use of the same movement, but give alternate explanations for the technique. Thus, I attempt to develop the techniques in which kicking motions are utilized in ways other than the obvious manner.

179

180

181

182

In this particular application, your opponent has grabbed your left wrist with his left hand (Figure 182). Once grabbed, your wrist begins to turn your body in a counterclockwise manner. This will help to remove your body from a possible punch to the head. As you turn your body, re-grab your opponent's wrist with your left hand; at the same time you can use the knuckles of your right fist to apply pressure to a point just above your opponent's elbow. This point is approximately one inch from the tip of your opponent's elbow. At this location, you will find Golgi tendon pressure receptors. Applying pressure to this location will enable you to elicit a reflex that causes the muscles to momentarily relax. This is known as the "Golgi tendon reflex." This reflex is a defensive mechanism of the body to save muscles and tendons from being ripped (Figure 183).

Once your opponent's arm has been rotated and you're able to apply pressure down on the elbow (Figure 184), execute a crescent kick with your right leg over the top of your opponent's left arm (Figure 185).

While you maintain your grip with your left hand, use your right leg to force your opponent to the ground. This type of technique will allow you to apply a great deal of force to your opponent's elbow. Not only can you use the strength of your leg to apply pressure, but you can also use your body weight to force your opponent to the ground (Figure 186).

In the final position of this technique, you can use your right hammer fist to strike the back of your opponent (Figure 188). Targets of opportunity that you should pay particular attention to are the kidneys, or it may be possible to strike Gallbladder 20. Of course, during the execution of this technique, you may find other strikes available to you. For example, as you begin to raise your leg up and over your opponent's arm, your right foot could kick the leg, the side of your opponent's body, or even the arm, for you to apply the takedown. Conceptually this is an important consideration for the critical analysis of kata. At any point in the execution of a technique, you may find the opportunity to deliver a percussive technique or possibly a joint lock. You must always be aware of these opportunities and be prepared to utilize them.

183

184

185

186

Throwing Applications to Grappling Techniques in Kata - Pinan 5 — Juji Gatame from a Standing Position

Continuing with the idea that unbalanced or unstable positions in kata may represent grappling techniques, I would like to look at Pinan 5. In this kata, there is a short sequence of techniques that makes used of a jump followed by an "X-stance." Your hands are also crossed in X formation (Figure 189). Preceding this jump, you will have been in a position where your right back fist is about head level, and your left hand is in front of your chest (Figure 190).

You're facing your opponent; both you and your opponent have your right foot forward (Figure 191). This technique could be performed equally well if your opponent were to grab the right side of your body with his right hand.

Strike your opponent with the back of your forearm on Stomach 9 or another suitable point. At the same time, grip your opponent's right wrist with your left hand (Figure 192).

Provided the strike to Stomach 9 was effective, your opponent should be somewhat groggy if not completely knocked out. If he still maintains consciousness press down on his shoulder with your right hand and pull him forward with your left (Figure 193).

Raise your right leg over his head while maintaining the grip with both hands (Figure194). As you bring your right foot down, release the grip on your opponent's shoulder with your right hand.

Continue turning, and at the moment your right foot touches the mat, roll yourself forward over your right arm and allow your left leg to circle back in front of your opponent's face (this movement is not clearly shown in the photographs). As you land on your back your opponent's left arm will be between your legs (Figure 195).

Take your opponent's head to the mat with your left leg and cross your ankles, maintaining your grip on your opponent's wrist. To apply pressure to this arm bar, you must have your hips extremely close to your opponent's shoulders; push your hips up and pull down with your arms. Your opponent's palm should be facing the ceiling to ensure that his elbow is in a position for maximum efficiency of the arm bar. This arm bar is similar to *juji gatame* used in judo. This is an extremely efficient arm bar; with proper application it is possible to break or dislocate your opponent's elbow. The final movement is very similar to the lock described in Figures 176 and 177.

187

188

189

190

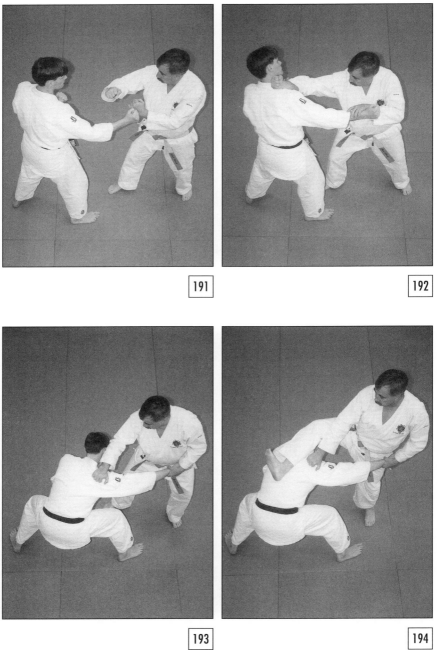

195

PINAN - HEIAN - PYUNG AHN 5

Pinan - Heian - Pyung Ahn 5 — Defense Against a Knee Kick from Grappling Range

In this sequence of techniques, I would like to consider responses we might reasonably expect to encounter. If your opponent grabs you by the neck and arm (Figure 196) and pulls your body forward and down, he is most likely to attack you by attempting to knee you in the head or face. As you're pulled forward, immediately drop your left arm into a position that could deflect his knee kick (Figure 197). After you have deflected his kick, raise your body so that your right forearm comes up and under his right arm (Figure 198). Slide your weight forward and continue pressing with your right forearm; at the same time strike Liver 13 or other targets of opportunity (Figure 199).

Liver 13 (Figure 200) is found at the tip of the eleventh rib. This is a very good point to attack; a strong attack to this point offers a possibility of a fracture to this rib. Some also believe that if you strike this point sufficiently hard, when the rib breaks, it could be driven into the kidney. If medical attention were not given to such an injury, infection could set in and could potentially be deadly.

196

197

198

199

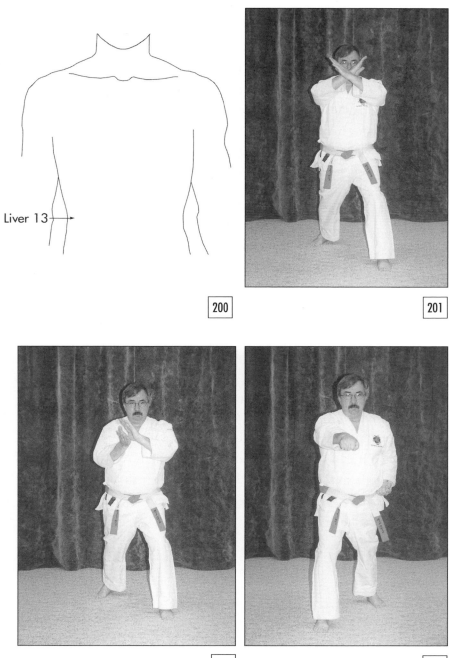

Liver 13

200

201

202

203

Timing of Hand Motions in Kata - Pinan 5 — X-block

Timing and execution of techniques in kata is an area that can give you considerable nuances to your bunkai. Take for example the "X-block" found in many kata. For the purposes of this book, I would like to use the short section found in Pinan 5. Depending on the style or system, the height and position of your hands will vary slightly, and the block will be followed immediately with a lung punch (Figures 201, 202, and 203). The way I've seen this technique taught, for the most part, is that the hands are brought up toward the head at the same time. That is to say neither the right nor the left hand arrives a split second prior to the other. As you might notice in this book, I tend to think in terms of "what if" rather than "this is the way it is." So let's look at a what-if situation. What if one hand were to be brought up a split second before the other hand. Would that give us a different perspective from which to view the technique and perhaps give us an alternate explanation? Remember, I believe firmly that there can be multiple explanations for any one technique in kata. Any bunkai you find useful or helpful is correct. I merely wish to offer some what-if bunkai, to stimulate your own thought processes. I truly hope that you will be able to take the bunkai I'm offering in this book and modify the techniques to fit your own particular needs.

In the following scenario, your opponent is facing you with his right foot forward, and you have your left foot forward (Figure 204). Your opponent punches with his left hand toward your face; simply raise your left hand to begin to deflect his punch (Figure 205). Immediately shoot your right hand up to and under your opponent's left wrist to begin to control your opponent's arm (Figure 206).

204

205

206

207

As you grab your opponent's wrist with your left hand, apply pressure to Heart 7 (Figure 209) with the base of your left forefinger (Figure. 207). You can complete this technique by punching a target of opportunity. One point that would be particularly effective would be Stomach 5 (Figure 210). This point is found in the front of the angle of the mandible and on the anterior border of the masseter muscle (Figure 210). This point if struck at a 45-degree angle down and in toward the body should dislocate the jaw, and would have a high probability of knocking out your opponent. This is an extremely effective point to strike and could present a great deal of danger to your opponent. So in practice you must be careful with this point.

208

Heart 7

209

Timing of Hand Motions in Kata - Jitte — Double Palm Heel Strike from a Cross-Hand Wrist Grab

Another technique that offers interesting alternate applications if we consider variations in the timing is the double palm heel strike. Like the X-block, this technique is typically performed with both hands striking at exactly the same time. The exact hand position can vary from system to system, but typically you find one hand at stomach level and the other around face level (Figure 211).

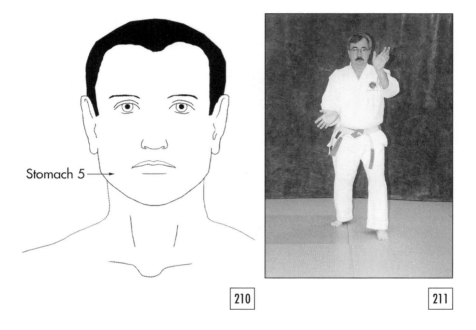

Stomach 5

210   211

If you observe closely when performing this technique, it seems as if your forward hand will arrive on target slightly before your opposite hand. If the individual who is performing this technique is sufficiently skilled and fast, it appears as if both hands will strike the target at exactly the same time. For the following situation I would like to make the assumption that your forward hand will be slightly ahead of the other; the way of your individual system may vary of course. As your opponent grabs your right wrist with his right hand (Figure 212), immediately turn your body slightly and rotate your right hand in a clockwise motion over the top of his grip (Figure 213). What you'll be attempting to do at this point is to apply an "S-lock," or *nikyo*, to your opponent's wrist (Figure 215). You should note that to attempt this lock with one hand is not as effective as using two hands. However, your intent and purpose in this technique is not to lock in control but to disrupt the balance of your opponent and to turn him to the side. If you can cause his legs to buckle slightly and turn away from you, it will make it more difficult for him to strike or kick you. To increase the effectiveness of this technique, once your opponent has grabbed your wrist, roll the back of your palm over his wrist. You want to press your hand forward toward his center line and imagine the energy in your arm to be spiraling up his arm (Figure 213).

212   213

214

If you can cause enough momentary pain to make your opponent's legs buckle and turn slightly away from you, targets of opportunity present themselves in the head and neck area. Any of these points, when struck with the palm of your hand should be able to knock out your opponent, or at least disrupt his balance to the point where other techniques could be utilized (Figure 214).

Timing of Hand Motions in Kata - Jitte - Shipsu — Preemptive Strike to the Head

The double-punch can be found in a number of kata (Figure 216). This technique is similar to the double palm heel strike in many respects. The major difference between these two techniques is the formation of the hand. In this technique, the striking surface appears to be your fist. Whereas in the previous example the palm heel delivered the percussive technique. Once again, one of the concepts I would like to look at is the timing of a particular technique. If we consider that one hand may arrive at the target before the other, there are a number of interesting bunkai possible.

215

216

In this situation, both you and your opponent have your right hand forward (Figure 217). Shift your position slightly forward by stepping with your right leg. At the same time, use the back of your forearm to strike your opponent on Large Intestine 11 (Figure 218). This should cause your opponent to drop his arm and expose the side of his neck. Multiple targets of opportunity can be exposed by this movement (Figure 219).

I believe that this concept of timing in a movement can be extremely important when you attempt to analyze kata. Even a slight delay of one hand motion can drastically alter your interpretation of the kata. I firmly believe that you should be able to vary the timing of particular moves in kata because it is virtually impossible to determine exactly how the creators of the various kata would have performed these movements.

217

These examples of bunkai are not the only explanation potentially available. Nor do I make the claim that these are the traditional bunkai that may have been taught by the old masters. These are simply techniques I have chosen to illustrate some concepts I feel are important. There are literally hundreds of techniques that could be used for these movements found in the various kata. It is my hope that these examples will provide you with some variations on techniques you know. Or, they may provide you with some inspiration to analyze your kata in such a way as to make the practice of kata more valuable to you. Kata are seen by many to be the central element of training in karate (or other percussive martial arts). With careful analysis of your kata, I am confident your understanding will deepen, and kata will take on a central role in your practice.

THE
POINTS

Attack where he is unprepared.

—Sun Tzu

This section of the book will be devoted to the location of points listed in the previous chapters. It is not to be taken as an inclusive list of all vital points, nor of all points used in acupuncture. I would suggest acquiring one or two good books that cover acupuncture and give detailed locations of the various points. In addition, I would recommend a good atlas of anatomy for the location of various muscles, nerves, tendons, organs, and bones. I would also suggest the purchase of *Textbook of Medical Physiology* by Guyton. I feel it is very important to have a professional library that covers various aspects of the martial arts. Since there are two paradigms by which vital points are discussed, it is important to have the resources at hand to follow the various points of view.

For the purposes of this book, I am using a measurement that is slightly different than what is used in traditional Chinese medicine. The location of points is normally measured by units called cuns. A cun is approximately one inch, and the way it was measured was to bend the tip of your index finger and use the distance between the first two joints as the unit of measurement. This distance will vary on each individual, yet it seems to give a good rule of thumb to locate points. But since every person is slightly different the location of the points will be slightly different. It takes some practice to be able to locate these points on different individuals, but it is possible to do so with a bit of determination. Also, since I tend to see measurements in terms of inches, it just makes more sense to use terms that are familiar.

Lung Points

1	Chungfu or Zhonfu
Location	Measure two inches from the nipple (in the direction of the arm). Count up three ribs. The point is between the first and second ribs from the top, one inch below the middle of the clavicle. One inch below the point Yun-men is the first intercostal space.

2	Yun-men
Location	Below the acromial extremity of the clavicle in the depression lateral to the triangle of m. pectoralis, six inches lateral to midline of the chest.

5	Chihtse/Chih Chai
Location	It is located on the cubital crease, on the radial side of the biceps brachii tendon.

5a	*This is not a traditional point used in Chinese acupuncture. It is, however, an additional point known as Tse sia*
Location	This point is approximately one inch down from Lung 5, and found in the "the valley" to the side of the biceps muscle.

6	Kungtsui/Kung Tsai/Kongzui
Location	Between brachioradial muscle and flexor carpi radialis on the radial side of the front of the forearm, seven inches above the wrist.

6a	*This is not a traditional point used in acupuncture.*
Location	This point is approximately one inch below Lung 6. It is found on the edge of the bone where the muscle curve meets the straight line of the radial bone.

7	Liehchueh/Lieque
Location	Open the person's thumb and index finger and slide his or her other hand into the space between them. His or her index finger should meet the point on the other wrist. Lung 7 is one and a half inches above the wrist fold.

8	Chingchu/Jingqu
Location	One inch above Taiyuan point on the radial side of the a. radialis.

9	Taiyuan
Location	Make a fist and bend at the wrist. Lung 9 is in the indentation of the first fold on the thumb side of the wrist, where a small pulse can be felt.

10	Yuchi / Yuji
Location	In the middle of the palmar surface of the os metacarpal 1, at the junction of the lighter and darker skin, by the thumb pad at the center of the first os metacarpal volaris.

11	Shaoshang
Location	On the radial side of the thumb, about one inch posterior to the corner of the nail.

LARGE INTESTINE POINTS

1	Shangyang
Location	On the radial side of the index finger, one inch posterior to the corner of the nail.

2	Erchien
Location	In the radial depression in front of the index finger joint; the point is located by loosely holding the fist.

3	Sanchien
Location	In the depression on the radial side of the index finger, posterior to the small head of the os metacarpal 2.

4	Hoku or Hegu
Location	At the midpoint of a line drawn from the web to the thumb to the confluence of the first and second metacarpal or at the proximal point of the crease formed by approximating the thumb and index finger.

5	Yanghsi or Yangxi
Location	With the thumb hyperextended, the point is located in the center of the depression bordered by the tendons of the extensor pollicius longus and brevis, and immediately distal to the styloid process of the radius. It is often called the anatomical snuff box.

10	Shousanli
Location	Measure three fingers' width down the forearm from the tip of the elbow crease on the outside.

11	Chuchin or Quchi
Location	On the outside of the upper arm just below the elbow, this point is found at the lateral end of the transverse cubital crease.

14	Pinao or Binao
Location	On the lateral aspect of the upper arm, slightly anterior to the insertion of m. deltoid on the line between point Tianyu and point Quchi (L.I. 11).

STOMACH POINTS

5	Daying
Location	Midline of the jaw, in facial artery groove.

9	Jengying or Jen Ying
Location	One-third of the way up the side of neck, located on both sides of the neck. With the thumb and middle finger of either hand, trace the crease line under your chin until you feel the larynx. Now press in and slightly away from the larynx. You will feel a pulse on one side of the Adam's apple, which marks the correct spot.

34	Liangchiu
Location	In the muscle that runs on the outside of the thigh, two inches up from the kneecap.

41	Chiehhsi or Jiexi
Location	In the center of the dorsal crease of the ankle joint, between the tendon of the m. extensor hallncis longus and the tendon of the m. extensor digit longus.

42	Chungyang
Location	One and a half inches distal to Jiexi (St. 41), at the highest spot of the dorsum of the foot.

43	Hsienku
Location	In the depression between the second and third os metatarsals.

44	Neiting
Location	One-half inch to the rear of the seam between the second and third toes.

45	Litui
Location	On the lateral side of the tip of the second toe, 0.1 inch posterior to the corner of the nail.

Spleen Points

1	Yinpai
Location	On the medial side of the great toe, 0.1 inch posterior to the corner of the nail.

2	Tatu
Location	On the medial side of the great toe, anterior and inferior to the first metatarsi-phalangeal joint, at the junction of the darker and lighter skin.

3	Taipai
Location	Below the posterior of the capitellum of the first metatarsal bone.

5	Shangchiu
Location	In the depression at the anterior-inferior border to the malleolus medialis.

6	Sanyinchaio or San yin jiao
Location	Approximately three inches above the tip of the medial malleolus, on the posterior border of the tibia.

9	Yinlingchuan or Yin ling quan
Location	Below the knee joint, on the medial margin of the musculus gastrocnemius, one finger width below the inner ankle of the tibia, where there is a depression.

10	Hsuehhai or Xue hai
Location	Have the person sit and bend his or her leg at a 90-degree angle. Catch the center of the kneecap with the center of your palm. The tip of your thumb will touch Spleen 10 two inches above the kneecap. It is on the inside of the leg.

12	Chungmen
Location	On the lateral side of the femoral artery, three and a half inches lateral to the midpoint of the superior border of the pubic symphysis.

21	Tapao or Dabao
Location	In the sixth intercostal space, on the midaxillary line.

HEART POINTS

2	Chingling
Location	Above the elbow, anterior; three inches above the elbow in the grove medial to m. biceps brachia.

3	Shaohai
Location	It is located at the medial end of the elbow crease.

3a	Extra Point
	This point is not used in traditional Chinese acupuncture.
Location	Located between Heart 5 and Heart 4. It is opposite Lung 6a and follows along the ulnar nerve.

4	Lingtao or Lingdao
Location	Anterior of wrist, approximately one inch above the crease of the wrist.

7	Shenmen
Location	In the crease on the side of the wrist nearest the little finger. Find the bony knob at the base of the outside of the palm. Have the person make a tight fist and bend the hand inward. Heart 7 is the small indentation below and slightly to the inside of the wrist bone.

8	Shaofu
Location	In the palm of the hand, toward the little finger, off-center. In the palmar surface, between the fourth and fifth metacarpal bones, just between the ring and small fingers when making a fist.

9	Shaochung or Shaochong
Location	On the radial side of the tip of the small finger, about a tenth of an inch posterior to the corner of the nail.

SMALL INTESTINE POINTS

1	Shaotse
Location	At the ulnar side of the small finger, about a tenth of an inch inch posterior to the corner of the nail.

2	Chienku
Location	In the depression anterior to the ulnar side of the fifth metacarpi-phalangeal joint. When a fist is formed, it is on the junction of the darker and lighter skin of the transverse crease, distal to the metacarpi-phalangeal joint.

3	Houhsi or Houxi
Location	On the fold that appears when the hand is making a fist, behind the little finger. Between the fourth and fifth fingers' metacarpals.

4	Wanku
Location	At the ulnar side of the border of the palm in the depression between the base of the fifth metacarpal bone and the trigonal bone.

Note: This point, if pressed, will relieve some of the pain associated with a strike to Heart 2.

5	Yangku
Location	At the ulnar side of the wrist in the depression between the styloid process of the ulna and the pisiform bone.

8	Hsiaohai or Shiao Hai
Location	At the elbow; in sulcus n. ulnar between the olecranon of the ulna and the epicondylus medialis of the humerus; flex the elbow when locating the point.

17	Tienjung
Location	At the mandible (base of the lower jaw). Located at the edge of the jaw, below and in front of the ears. Posterior to the angle of the lower jaw, in the depression on the anterior border of the m. sternocleido-mastoids.

BLADDER POINTS

40	Weichung or Weizhong
Location	This point is located on the back of the knee. It is to be found in the exact midpoint of the popliteal transverse crease.

57	Chengshan, Ch'eng-San (Cheng Shan)
Location	When you rise on the balls of the feet, the calf muscle will be easy to see. The point is found at the distal margin of the gastrocnemius muscle and between its medial and lateral heads.

60   Kunlun
Location   Middle point between the tip of malleolus lateralis and the
                    tendo calcaneus.

65   Shuku
Location   Posterior and inferior to the small head of the os metatar-
                    sale.

66   Tungku
Location   In the depression anterior and inferior to the fifth metatar-
                    sophalangae.

67   Chinhyin
Location   On the lateral side of the tip of the small toe, about a tenth
                    of an inch proximal to the corner of the nail.

KIDNEY POINTS

1   Yungchuan
Location   At the boundary between the anterior one-third and the
                    posterior two-thirds of the center line of the sole of the foot.

2   Janku or Rangu
Location   In the depression at the inferior border of the tuberositas
                    ossis navicularis.
                    Note: This point can be used as a katsu for a strike to the
                    testicles. You would strike with middle knuckle of your fist
                    in a direction up the leg. Then massage up the foot and up
                    the leg.

3   Taihsi
Location   On the inside of the anklebone one-half the distance between
                    the Achilles tendon and the tip of the anklebone.

10   Yinku

Location   It is found on the medial side of the knee joint between the
                   two tendons at the medial edge of the inner knee crease.

PERICARDIUM POINTS

3   Chutse or Quze

Location   In the transverse cubital crease, at the ulnar side of the ten-
                   don of m. biceps brachia; a slight flexion of the elbow helps
                   in locating this point.

4   Hsimen

Location   Five inches above the transverse crease of wrist, between the
                   tendons of m. palmaris longus and m. flexor carpi radialis.

5   Chienshih

Location   Three inches above the transverse crease of the wrist, be-
                   tween the tendons of m. palmaris longus and m. flexor carpi
                   radialis.

7   Taling or Daling

Location   At the midpoint of the transverse crease of the wrist between
                   the tendons of m. palmaris longus and m. flexor carpi radia-
                   lis.

8   Laokung or Laongong

Location   When the four fingers are bent to touch the palm, the point
                   is between the tips of the middle and ring fingers.

9   Chungchung

Location   In the center of the tip of the middle finger.

TRIPLE WARMER POINTS

1	Kuachung or Guanchong
Location	On the ulnar side of the ring finger, a tenth of an inch posterior to corner of nail.

2	Yemen
Location	In the web between the ring and the small finger.

3	Chungchu or Zongzhu
Location	Clench the hand when locating this point, which is between the ossa metacarpale IV and V, in the depression one inch above the art. metacarpophalengeae.

6	Chihkou or Zhigou
Location	One inch above Waiguan (TW 5), between the ulna and the radius.

10	Tienching Tianjing
Location	Superior to the olecranon, in the depression when the elbow is flexed.

13	Naohui
Location	Three inches below Jianliao (TW 14) at the posterior border of m. deltoideus.

16	Tienyu or Tianyou
Location	Behind the ear and down one inch. Posterior and inferior to the mastoid process, on the posterior border of sternocleidomastoideus, at the level of the angle of the mandible.

17	Yifeng or Ersha or Tianzon
Location	This point is located in the mastoid cavity below the ears.

GALLBLADDER POINTS

20	Fengchih
Location	This point is located 1 inch above the hairline, on the sides of the big muscles in the neck, next to the greater occipital nerve, where it arches over the occiput.

31	Fengshih
Location	On the upper thigh outside, halfway up the external side of the thigh. On the side of the thigh at the tip of the middle finger when the arms are straight down—the point is below the tip of the middle finger.

32	Chungtu or Femur-Zhondu
Location	Two inches under GB 31.

38	Yangfu
Location	Four inches above the tip of the external malleolus, on the anterior border of the fibula.

41	Linchi
Location	Between the fifth and fourth Metatarsal (little toe) in the middle. Measure two fingers' width up from the bridge between the fourth and fifth toes.

42	Tiwuhui or Diwuhiu
Location	Between the ossa metatarsalia 4 and 5, a half inch anterior to pt. Foot-Linqi (GB 41).

43	Hsiahsi or Xiaxi
Location	On the cleft between the fourth and fifth metatarsal bones, a half inch proximal to the margin of the web.

44   Chiaoyin or Qiaoyin

Location   On the lateral side of the tip of the fourth toe, a tenth of an inch posterior to the corner of the nail.

Liver Points

1   Tatun

Location   On the lateral aspect of the dorsum of the terminal phalanx of the big toe, midway between the lateral corner of the nail and the interphalangeal joint.

2   Hsingchien or Xingjian

Location   Half an inch proximal to the margin of the web between the first and second toes.

3   Taichung or Taichong

Location   On the dorsum of the foot between the ossa metatarsale I and II, in the depression posterior to the art. metatarso-phalange. Between the first and second toe, two inches proximal to the margin of the web.

4   Chungfeng or Zhongteng

Location   Halfway between the front edge of the anklebone and the stringy muscles at the top of the foot.

8   Chuchuan or Quguan

Location   Approximately four inches above the medial epicondylus of the femur, between the vastus medialis and the sartorius muscle.

13   Changmen or Zhangmen

Location   Between the eleventh and twelfth floating ribs at the lower border of the free end of the eleventh rib.

CONCEPTION VESSEL

| 6 | Chihai, Daintien or Tan tien |
| Location | One and one-half inch below the navel. |

| 15 | Chiuwei or Jiuwei or Hsinkan |
| Location | At the solar plexus, a half inch inferior to the xiphoid process. |

| 24 | Chengchiang or Cheng Chian |
| Location | Below the lip and above chin, one index finger's width inferior to the mucocutaneous line of the lower lip at the symphysis menti, or below the midpoint of the lower lip. |

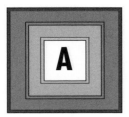

APPENDIX A:
VITAL POINTS LISTS

On the following pages, you will find various lists with the names of vital points. These lists come from a number of sources. Some are no longer in print, others are from private collection, and others are currently in print. Finding charts with the location of vital points is not a difficult task; what is difficult is to find instruction on how to make use of these points. Of equal or greater value is learning how to practice these techniques in a safe and sensible manner. Remember, unless you are under the supervision of an instructor who has trained in vital-point techniques and revival techniques, do not strike these points. It is relatively safe to locate these points by pushing or grabbing. In fact, you can get a good idea of the effectiveness of these points by applying strong pressure with a grab or a push. This will give you the opportunity to practice locating vital points quickly and accurately. Then, when you practice, you will find your hand instinctively going to these points.

ANTERIOR VITAL POINTS: SAIKO, ET AL. (1972)

1	Tento	renversement du ciel
2	Choto	oiseau-livre
3	Kasumi	brouillard
4	Gekon	crepuscule
5	Zenshakutaku	petit etang avant
6	Wakikage	ombre de l'aisselle
7	Inazuma	eclair
8	Yako	lumiere nocturne
9	Fukuto	lievre agite
10	Mukobone	devant du tibia
11	Kori	ecaille pointue
12	Uchi Kurubushi	cheville interieure
13	Sobi	fronttement de l'herbe
14	Tsurigane	cloche
15	Tsukikage	ombre de la lune
16	Uchiro Shakutaku	petit etang arriere
17	Shoho	petit carre
18	Tanchu	centre de l'homme
19	Jinchu	centre de l'homme
20	Ryomo	deux poils

POSTERIOR VITAL POINTS: SAIKO, ET AL. (1972)

1	Tendo	voie du ciel
2	Dokko	ciel unique
3	Denko	lumiere irradiante
4	Ushiro Inazuma	eclair arriere
5	Soto Kurubushi	cheville exterieure
6	Soobi	frottement de l'herbe
7	Ushiro Zume	point arriere ecrase
8	Kibi	queue de tortue
9	Hijizuen	point ouvert
10	Shuko	carapace de la main
11	Kayaku	point ouvert
12	Ushiro Shakutaku	petit etang arriere
13	Wanjun	bras domestique
14	Hayauchi	coup rapide

VITAL POINTS OF HISATAKA (1976)

1	Tento	top of the head
2	Miken	pineal gland
3	Bito	bridge of the nose
4	Bisen	base of the nose
5	Kasumi	temples
6	Gankyu	eyeballs
7	Jinchu	upper lip
8	Kagaku	lower part of the jaw
9	Mikazuki	mandible, base of the lower jaw
10	Ryo jikou kabotoke	mastoid
11	Nodo botoke	adam's apple
12	Keido myakubu or matsukaze	jugular vein area or carotid artery
13	Hichu	neck's notch
14	Kyokotsu	sternum
15	Kyosen	xiphoid process
16	Tanchu	sternal angle
17	Ganka	Rib cage right below the nipples
18	Rokkotsu or Denko	rib cage area
19	Mizo ochi or Suigetsu	solar plexus
20	Kafuku bu or Tanden	lower abdomen

VITAL POINTS OF HISATAKA (1976) *CONTINUED*

21	Kinteki	testicles
22	Inazuma	side of the stomach
23	Yako	inguinal region
24	Fushito	outside thigh
25	Shitsu to	knee cap
26	Keikotsu or Kokei	tibia
27	Sokko	instep
28	Hijitsume	elbow
29	Haisu	back of the hand
30	Kassatsu	spine
31	Kotobu	back of the head
32	Keichu	back of the neck
33	Ushiro rokkotsu or ushiro denko	kidneys
34	Kibi	spine tip
35	Hiza kubomi	back side of the knee
36	Kuru bushi	ankle

VITAL POINTS OF FUNAKOSHI (1973)

1	Tendo	coronal suture
2	Tento	frontal fontanel
3	Kasumi	temple
4	Seidon	circumorbital region
5	Gansei	eyeball
6	Uto	glabella
7	Jinchu	intermaxillary suture
8	Gekon	center of lower jaw
9	Mikazuki	base of mandible
10	Matsukaze	side of neck
11	Hichu	suprasternal notch
12	Tanchu	sternal angle
13	Kyosen	xiphoid process
14	Murasame	supraclavicular fossa
15	Suigetsu	solar plexus
16	Myojo or Tanden	point about one inch below the umbilicus
17	Kyoei	subaxillary region
18	Ganka	region below the nipples
19	Denko	hypochondriac region
20	Inazuma	lumbar region
21	Uchi Shakutaku	inside of the wrist
22	Shuko	back of the hand
23	Yako	inguinal region
24	Fukuto	lateral part of the lower thigh

VITAL POINTS OF FUNAKOSHI (1973) *CONTINUED*

25	Naike, Uchikurubushi, or Uchikurobushi	medial malleolus
26	Kori	instep
27	Soin or Kusagakure	top lateral part of the foot
28	Kokotsu or mukozune	middle of the fibula
29	Kinteki	testes
30	Dokko	concavity behind the ear
31	Keichu	back of the neck
32	Hayauchi	middle of the scapular ridge
33	Kassatsu	space between the 5th and 6th thoracic vertebrae
34	Ushiro denko	left and right sides of the 9th and 11th vertebrae
35	Bitei	tip of the spine
36	Wanjun	dorsal surface of the upper arm
37	Chukitsu or Hijizume	lateral surface of the elbow
38	Sotoshakutaku	dorsal surface of the wrist between the radius and ulna
39	Ushiro inazuma	gluteal fold
40	Kusanagi	lower part of the soleus muscle

VITAL POINTS OF E.J. HARRISON (1959)

1	Tendo	crown of the head
2	Tento	the fontanelle or space between the crown of the head and forehead
3	Komekami	the temple
4	Mimi	the ears
5	Miken	summit of nose in center of forehead
6	Seidon	area above and below the eyes
7	Gansei	eyeballs
8	Jinchu	philtrum or spot just under the nose
9	Gekon	spot beneath the lower lip
10	Mikazuki	the jaw
11	Dokko	mastoid process behind the ears
12	Keichu	nape of the neck
13	Shofu	side of the neck
14	Sonu	spot between throat and top of breastbone or sternum
15	Hichu	base of throat, Adam's apple or projection of the thyroid cartilage of the larynx
16	Danchu	summit of breastbone or sternum

VITAL POINTS OF E.J. HARRISON *CONTINUED*

17	Kyototsu	base of breastbone or sternum
18	Suigetsu	solar plexus
19	Kyoei	below the armpits, approximately the spot between the 5th and 6th ribs
20	Ganchu	spot below the nipples
21	Denko	spot between the 7th and 8th ribs
22	Inazuma	side of the body slightly above the hips
23	Myojo	spot about an inch below the navel
24	Soda	spot between shoulder blades
25	Katsusatsu	spot between the 5th and 6th vertebra
26	Kodenko	base of spine
27	Wanshun	back of arm, top of outside edge of upper arm
28	Hijizume	elbow joint
29	Udekansetsu	arm joint
30	Kote	wrist or back of lower forearm
31	Uchijakuzawa or Miyakudokoro	inner parts of the forearm where pulsation can be felt

VITAL POINTS OF E.J. HARRISON *CONTINUED*

32	Sotojakuzawa	opposite side to Uchijakuzawa
33	Shuko	back of the hand
34	Kinteki	testicles
35	Yako	inside of upper thigh
36	Fukuto	outside of lower part of thigh
37	Hizakansetsu	knee joint
38	Kokotsu	center point of the tibia (shin-bone) and fibula (splint bone on outer side of leg)
39	Uchikurobushi	inside of ankle joint
40	Kori	upper surface of instep
41	Kusagakure	outside edge of top of the foot
42	Bitei	the coccyx, i.e. small triangular bone ending human spinal column
43	Ushiro Inazuma	spot below the buttocks
44	Sobi	spot on inside of lower part of leg, approximately base of calf

VITAL POINTS OF YOKOYAMA AND OSHIMA (1915)

1	Tento	top of the head
2	Kasumi	temple
3	Jinchu	intermaxillary suture
4	Murasame	supraclavicular fossa
5	Hichu	suprasternal notch
6	Danchu	summit of breastbone or sternum
7	Ganchu	spot below the nipples
8	Tsukikage	the left side somewhere about the lowest rib
9	Myojo	point about on inch below the umbilicus
10	Uto	glabella
11	Matsukaze	side of neck
12	Shoho	spot about 2 inches below Hichu
13	Suigetsu	solar plexus
14	Denko	the right side somewhere about the lowest rib
15	Tsurigane	testes

VITAL POINTS OF CASEY (1984)

1	Yang pai	top center of skull slightly behind the hairline
2	Han yen	spot between the outer corner of the eye, and upper part of ear, where joins the skull
3	Hsuan lu	temple
4	Tsuan chu	between the eyebrows
5	Szu pai	directly under the eye on the cheekbone
6	Hsuan chi	the hollow of the throat
7	Chian	center of the lower jaw
8	T'ien yu	the area about the sternocleidomastoid muscle
9	Jen ying	either side of the larynx just under the angle of the jawbone
10	Chueh p'en	the nerve centers in the back of the collarbone
11	Hua kai Tzu kung Yu t'ang Shang chung Chung ting	the cartilage covering the ribs where they join the sternum
12	Chi wei	the area under the solar plexus
13	Ch'i hai	about three inches below the navel

VITAL POINTS OF CASEY (1984) *CONTINUED*

14	Yi hsi	under the armpit between the 4th and 5th rib
15	Pu lang	on the side, on a horizontal line with the base of the sternum, between the ribs
16	Chi shi	at the side, a point half way between the hip bone and lower rib and in a vertical line with the center of the thigh
17	San yang lo	on the wrist about one inch above the distal end of the humerus and ulna bones
18	Lao kung	inside the wrist one inch above the base of the palm and slightly toward the ulnar side
19	Yin lien	the inside of the thigh on a level with the lower part of the scrotum, slightly to the front of the thigh
20	Feng shi	outside of the thigh halfway between the knee and hip
21	Chung feng	a point just below and slightly forward of the medial malleolus
22	Nei t'ing	the instep between the 1st and 2nd toes about one and one half inch above the joint

VITAL POINTS OF CASEY (1984) *CONTINUED*

23	Yung ch'uan	the bottom of the foot about 2 inches back of the ball and close to the inner edge
24	Chi hsu	the nerve just under the lateral malleolus
25	Wan ku	the base of the skull
26	Feng ch'ih	back of the neck between the 3rd and 4th vertebrae
27	Ta ch'ui	a point one inch to the right or left of the 7th cervical vertebra

VITAL POINTS OF GRUZANSKI (1968)

1	Tendo	crown of the head
2	Tento	the fontanelle or space between the crown of the head and the forehead
3	Komekami	the temple
4	Mimi	the ears
5	Seidon	area above and below the eyes
6	Miken	nasion or summit of the nose in the center of the forehead
7	Gansei	eyeballs
8	Jinchu	the philtrum or spot just under the nose
9	Gekon	spot beneath the lower lip
10	Mikazuki	the jaw
11	Hichu	base of the throat, Adam's apple or projection of the thyroid cartilage of the larynx
12	Danchu	summit of the breastbone or sternum
13	Donu	spot between the throat and top of the breastbone or sternum
14	Kyototsu	the base of the breastbone or sternum
15	Suigetsu	the solar plexus

VITAL POINTS OF GRUZANSKI (1968) *CONTINUED*

16	Kyoei	below the armpits, between the 5th and 6th ribs
17	Inazuma	side of the body, slightly above the hips
18	Ganchu	spot below the nipples
19	Myojo	spot about an inch below the navel
20	Denko	spot between the 7th and 8th ribs
21	Kinteki	testicles
22	Yako	inside of upper thigh
23	Fukuto	outside of lower part of the thigh
24	Hizakansetsu	knee joint
25	Kokotsu	the center point of the tibia or shinbone
26	Uchikurobushi	inside of the ankle joint
27	Kori	upper surface of the instep
28	Kusagakkure	top outer edge of the foot
29	Dokko	the mastoid process or spot behind the ear
30	Keichu	nape of the neck
31	Shofu	side of the neck
32	Soda	spot between the shoulder blades

VITAL POINTS OF GRUZANSKI (1968) *CONTINUED*

33	Wanshun	back of arm, top of outside edge of upper arm
34	Katsusatsu	spot below 'soda'
35	Jinzo	kidney
36	Hijizume	elbow joint
37	Kanzo	liver
38	Udekansetsu	arm joint
39	Kote	wrist or back of the lower forearm
40	Kodenko	base of the spine
41	Bitei	the coccyx, small triangular bone ending human spinal column
42	Sotojakuzawa	outer portion of the forearm
43	Uchijakuzawa or Miyakudokoro	inner parts of the forearm where pulsation can be felt
44	Shuko	back of the hand
45	Ushiro Inazuma	spot below the buttocks
46	Sobi	spot on inside of the lower part of the leg, at the base of the calf
47	Akiresuken	Achilles tendon

Vital Points of Choi (1965)

1	Taesinmun	skull
2	Migan	bridge of nose
3	Angom	eyelid
4	Anbu	eyes
5	Injung	philtrum
6	Moktongmaek	neck artery
7	T'ok	point of chin
8	Soegol sang'wa	clavicle
9	Kyolhu	Adam's apple
10	Sumt'ong	windpipe
11	Kasum	chest
12	Sonmok	wrist
13	Myongch'i	solar plexus
14	Chonggwong	ribs
15	p'almok kwanjol	elbow joint
16	Hyoppok	floating ribs
17	Habokpu	abdomen
18	Nangsim	groin
19	Ch'ibu	inner thighs
20	Kyonggol	shins
21	Palttung	insteps
22	Kwanjanori	temple
23	Huibu	ear points
24	Polttagwi	jaw

VITAL POINTS OF CHOI (1965) *CONTINUED*

25	Witmok	upper neck
26	Kyon kap	upper back
27	Kyodurang	armpits
28	Kyong ch'u	small of the back
29	K'ong p'at	kidney
30	Ansonmok	inner wrist
31	Mijobu	coccyx
32	Ogum	hollow of knee
33	Murup Kwanjol	leg joint
34	Changttanji	calf
35	Twitch'uk yakchom	Achilles tendon

VITAL POINTS OF HASHIMOTO (1964)

1	Suigetsu	solar plexus
2	Hichu	suprasternal notch
3	Tanchu	sternal angle
4	Tanden	point about one inch below the umbilicus
5	Ganka	region below the nipples
6	Inazuma	lumbar region
7	Tento	top of the head
8	Doko	concavity behind the ear
9	Kasumi	temple
10	Seidon	area above the below the eyes
11	Jinchu	philtrum or spot just under the nose
12	Gekon	center of lower jaw
13	Mikazuki	the jaw
14	Uchi Shakutaku	inside of the wrist
15	Soto Shakutaku	outside of the wrist
16	Shuko	back of the hand
17	Fukuto	lateral part of the lower thigh
18	Uchikurobushi	inside of ankle joint
19	Kori	upper surface of instep

VITAL POINTS OF HASHIMOTO (1964) *CONTINUED*

20	Kusagakure	outside edge of top of the foot
21	Ushiro Inazuma	spot below the buttocks
22	Kusanagi	lower part of the soleus muscle
23	Hayauchi	middle of scapular ridge
24	Kassatsu	space between the 5th and 6th thoracic vertebrae
25	Bitei	tip of the spine

VITAL POINTS OF HANCOCK (1904)

1	Lower leg	across the shin on either side, and well to the front, strike half-way up the lower leg
2	Upper leg	strike half way between knee and trunk, either across front of leg, or at outside of leg somewhat to the front
3	Side Blow	squarely on either side of the lower trunk, in the soft part just below the last rib
4	Kidney	strike over this organ in small of back, in soft part just below last rib
5	Fore-arm	on either side, half way between wrist and elbow
6	Upper arm	strike across front of biceps, or on outside of arm and well to the front; in either case point of striking to be midway between elbow and shoulder
7	Collarbone	on collarbone midway between breast bond and point of shoulder
8	Shoulder	midway between neck and point of shoulder
9	Side of the neck	midway between jaw-bone and collarbone
10	Base of spine	*this point is listed as too dangerous to use

VITAL POINTS OF YAE KICHI YABE (1904)

1	Ryo Jikou Kabotoke	cavity below the eres
2	Keichu	back of the neck
3	Kassatsu	spine, between the 5th and 6th vertebrae
4	Ushikro Denko	kidneys
5	Kibi	tip of the spine
6	Jinchu	upper lip
7	Kagaku	tip of the jaw
8	Mikazuke	base of the lower jaw
9	Matsukaze	side of the neck at the carotid artery
10	Kyokotu, kyosen, or tanchu	solar plexus
11	Kinteki	testicles
12	Ude	on either side of forearm, half way between wrist and elbow

VITAL POINTS OF WU (1990)

1	Taiyang	24	Fengfu
2	Erqiao	25	Fengchi
3	Yanhou	26	Yamen
4	Yasai	27	Tiantu
5	Jianjing	28	Xinkan
6	Xuanji	29	Shaohai
7	Jiangtai	30	Quze
8	Qimen	31	Quchi
9	Zhangmen	32	Gongsun
10	Neiguan	33	Rugen
11	Hegu	34	Zhubin
12	Xinkan	35	Weizhong
13	Taichong	36	Fengyan
14	Wanmai	37	Rudong
15	Binao	38	Beiliang
16	Jugu	39	Jingchu
17	Dantian	40	Xiaoyao
18	Danzhong	41	Weilong
19	Huiyin	42	Beixin
20	Yongquan	43	Yanggu
21	Baihiu	44	Yangchi
22	Ermen	45	Fengwei
23	Tianrong	46	Tianrong

VITAL POINTS OF KANO (1937)

1	Tendo	7	Suigetsu
2	Kasumi	8	Getsuei
3	Uto	9	Denko
4	Dokko	10	Myojo
5	Jinchu	11	Tsurigane
6	Kachikake	12	Shitsukansetsu

VITAL POINTS OF COSNECK (1944)

1	Upper lip	14	Tissue over eyes
2	Temple and ears	15	Hollow of armpit
3	Wrist or bones of thumb	16	Behind ear lobe
4	Biceps muscles	17	Tissue between jawbone and throat
5	Testicles	18	Calf
6	Adam's apple	19	Sides of spine
7	Kidneys	20	Pectoral or arm pit
8	Collar bone	21	Solar plexus
9	Sides of jaw	22	Ears
10	Temple bones	23	Instep
11	Bridge of nose	24	Nostrils
12	Back of neck		
13	Throat below Adam's apple		

VITAL POINTS OF TRIAS (1980)

1	Top of skull	25	Groin
2	Bone above eyes	26	Front of thigh
3	Eyeballs	27	Knee cap
4	Bridge of nose	28	Shin
5	Under nose	29	Inner and outer ankle
6	Jaw	30	Instep
7	Under lower lip	31	Base of skull
8	Side of neck	32	Behind ears
9	Adam's apple	33	Carotid artery, side of neck
10	Throat		
11	Collar bone	34	7th vertebrae
12	Upper breast bone	35	Trapezius muscle
13	Between 5th and 6th rib	36	Between top of shoulder blades
14	Biceps	37	Back of upper arm
15	Under breast nipple	38	Kidney
16	Lower breast bone	39	Small of back
17	Between 7th and 8th rib	40	Back of forearm
		41	Tailbone
18	Spleen	42	Back of hand
19	Solar plexus	43	Back of thigh
20	Floating rib	44	Inner and outer side of knee
21	Below navel		
22	Outer forearm	45	Calf of leg
23	Inner wrist	46	Back of heel
24	Bladder	47	Bottom of foot

VITAL POINTS OF WANG (1983)

1	Baihui	12	Dantian
2	Xuanguan	13	Mingmen
3	Yuzhen	14	Huantiao
4	Jianjin	15	Weilu
5	Jiaji	16	Huiyin
6	Shanzhong	17	Fengshi
7	Quchi	18	Yanglingquan
8	Chize	19	Yinlingquan
9	Shaohai	20	Yongquan
10	Neilaongong	21	Yifeng
11	Wailaogong		

APPENDIX B:
BIBLIOGRAPHY

Applegate, R. *Kill or Get Killed*, Military Services Publishing Co.: Harrisburg, PA (1943).

Baxendale, R. H., Conway, B.A., Ferrell, W.R. "Conditioning of crossed extensor reflex pathways by independent natural stimulation of labyrinth, neck and elbow joint afferents," *Brain Res.*, 377 (1986) 41–6.

Berry, J. "Discussion on the Diagnosis and Treatment of Injuries of the Intestines." *British Medical Journal* 2:643 (1921).

Casey, C. G., *Chinese Mind-Hit Boxing: Secrets of Kai Sai Kung Fu (A study in Esoteric Energy Methods)*, Kyoshu Mission (1984).

Choi, H. H. *Taekwon-Do: The Art of Self-Defense*, Daeha Publications Co.: Seoul (1965).

Cosneck, B. J. *American Combat Judo*, Sentinel Books Arts Crafts Sports Education: New York (1944).

Fairbairn, W. E. *Hands Off! Self-Defense for Women*, D. Appleton-Century Co., Inc.: New York/London (1942).

Funakoshi, G. *Karate-Do Kyohan: The Master Text*, Kodansha International Ltd.: Tokyo (1973).

Funakoshi, G. *Karate-Do Nyumon: The Master Introductory Text*, Kodansha International Ltd.: Tokyo (1988).

Gruzanski, C. V. *Spike and Chain: Japanese Fighting Arts*, Charles E. Tuttle Co.: Rutland, VT (1968).

Guyton, A. C. *Textbook of Medical Physiology*, W. B. Saunders Co.: Philadelphia, London, Toronto, Mexico City, Rio de Janeiro, Sydney, Tokyo, Hong Kong (1986).

Hancock, H. I. *Jiu-Jutsu Combat Tricks: Japanese Feats of Attack and Defense in Personal Encounters*, G.P. Putnam's Sons: New York (1904).

Hancock, H. I. *The Complete Kano Jiu-Jitsu (Judo)*, G.P. Putnam's Sons: New York/ London (1905).

Harrison, E. J. *The Manual of Karate*, W. Foulsham & Co. Ltd.: New York (1959).

Hisataka, M. *Scientific Karatedo*, Japan Publications, Inc.: Tokyo (1976).

Hunter, H. H. *Super Ju-Jutsu* (1938).

Jokl, E. *The Medical Aspect of Boxing*, J. L. Van Schik, Limited: Pretoria (1941).

Jorgensen, S. J. *Thirty-six Secret Knock-out Blows without the Use of Fists*, Seattle, WA (1930).

Kaku, K. *Yasuhiro Konishi: Karate and His Life*, (1993) by Yasuhiro Konishi.

Kano, J. *Judo: Jujutsu*, Maruzen Company Ltd.: Tokyo (1937).

Kaptchuk, T. J. *The Web That Has No Weaver: Understanding Chinese Medicine*, Congdon & Weed: New York (1983).

Leggett, T. *The Spirit of Budo; Old Traditions for Present Day Life*, The Simul Press, Inc.: Tokyo (1993).

Longhurst, P. *Jiu-Jitsu and Other Methods of Self-Defense*, L. Upcott Gill: London (approx. 1900).

Munro, D. *Cranio-Cerebral Injuries*. London (1938).

Musashi, M. *A Book of Five Rings*, translated by Victor Harris, The Overlook Press: Woodstock, NY (1974).

Nakayama, M. *Best Karate Vol. 5 (Heian, Tekki)*, Kodansha: Tokyo (1979).

Otsuka, H. *Wado Ryu Karate*, translated by Shingo Ishida, Master Publication: Hamilton, Canada (Original book written in 1977).

Phelps, W. M. *The Control of Football Injuries*, A.S. Barnes and Company: New York (1933).

Saiko, F., Plee H., Devevere, J. *Les Points: Vitaux Secrets du Corps Humain*, Judo International: Paris (1972).

Smith, R. W. *Chinese Boxing: Masters and Methods*, North Atlantic Books: Berkeley, CA (1974).

Training Division Bureau of Aeronautics U.S. Navy. *Hand to Hand Combat*, United States Naval Institute: Annapolis, MD (1943).

Trias, R. A. *The Pinnacle of Karate*, Self Published (1980).

Wang, P., Zeng, W. *Wu Style Taijiquan,* Hai Feng Publishing Co.: Hong Kong (1983).

Wu, J. *Chinese Kung* Fu Series: 72 Consummate Arts Secrets of the Shaolin Temple: *Compiled by Wu Jiaming*, translated by Rou Gang, revised by Yang Yinrong, Fujian Science and Technology Publishing House: Fujian (1990).

Yabe, Y. K. *Jiu-Jutsu: The Japanese National System of Physical Training and Self-Defense*, Clark, Dudley & Co.: Rochester, NY (1904).

Yerkow, C. *Modern Judo: Basic Technique* (vol. 1), The Military Service Publishing Co.: Harrisburg, PA (1947).

Yokoyama, S., Oshima, E. *Judo*, Nishodo, Japan (1915).

"Books to Span the East and West"

Tuttle Publishing was founded in 1832 in the small New England town of Rutland, Vermont [USA]. Our core values remain as strong today as they were then—to publish best-in-class books which bring people together one page at a time. In 1948, we established a publishing office in Japan—and Tuttle is now a leader in publishing English-language books about the arts, languages and cultures of Asia. The world has become a much smaller place today and Asia's economic and cultural influence has grown. Yet the need for meaningful dialogue and information about this diverse region has never been greater. Over the past seven decades, Tuttle has published thousands of books on subjects ranging from martial arts and paper crafts to language learning and literature—and our talented authors, illustrators, designers and photographers have won many prestigious awards. We welcome you to explore the wealth of information available on Asia at **www.tuttlepublishing.com**.

Published by Tuttle Publishing, an imprint of Periplus Editions (HK) Ltd.

www.tuttlepublishing.com

Copyright © 2001 Bernard Richard Clark

Library of Congress Cataloging-in-Publication Data

Clark, Rick, 1948-
    Pressure point fighting / Rick Clark
        194 p. ill; 23 cm
        Includes bibliographical references.
        ISBN 0-8048-3217-X (pb)
    GV1114.3.C52 2001
    796.815/3—dc21
        99059666

ISBN 978-0-8048-5434-4

25 24 23 22 21
5 4 3 2 1   2110VP

Printed in Malaysia

Distributed by:

**North America,
Latin America & Europe**
Tuttle Publishing
364 Innovation Drive
North Clarendon,
VT 05759-9436 U.S.A.
Tel: 1 (802) 773-8930
Fax: 1 (802) 773-6993
info@tuttlepublishing.com
www.tuttlepublishing.com

Japan
Tuttle Publishing
Yaekari Building, 3rd Floor,
5-4-12 Osaki, Shinagawa-ku
Tokyo 141 0032
Tel: (81) 3 5437-0171
Fax: (81) 3 5437-0755
sales@tuttle.co.jp
www.tuttle.co.jp

Asia Pacific
Berkeley Books Pte. Ltd.
3 Kallang Sector #04-01
Singapore 349278
Tel: (65) 6741-2178
Fax: (65) 6741-2179
inquiries@periplus.com.sg
www.tuttlepublishing.com

TUTTLE PUBLISHING® is a registered trademark of Tuttle Publishing, a division of Periplus Editions (HK) Ltd.